THE JAMES BOND GIRLS

WRITTEN & DESIGNED BY
GRAHAM RYE

A Citadel Press Book
Published by Carol Publishing Group

W9-BZO-477

Graham Rye is the author and designer of *The James Bond Girls*. His fascination with the James Bond character began in 1962 when his father took him to see the film *Dr. No* at the age of eleven. His interest has persisted over the years, and as President of The James Bond 007 International Fan Club & Archive he produces 007-related publications which are read in over 40 countries world wide.

In researching the pictures for this book, he has attempted to compile a collection of photographs which prove to be the definitive portfolio on the James Bond Girls.

The James Bond 007 International Fan Club & Archive can be contacted at PO Box 007 · Addlestone · Surrey · KT15 1DY · England

For Lee - every inch a Bond Girl

The publishers would like to point out that each film's cast and credit lists are selective and do not, in any way, represent full credit listings.

The publishers would like to thank John Parkinson, Andrew Pilkington and Tim Greaves for their invaluable assistance in the creation of this book.

Many photographers covered the Bond sets over the years. To pay them tribute, we mention the following few: Graham Attwood, Bert Cann, Albert Clarke, Frank Connor, Loomis Dean, Arthur Evans, Greg Gorman, Keith Hamshere, Ray Hearne, David Hurn, David James, Peter Kernot, Douglas Kirkland, Herman Leonard, Patrick Morin, Terry O'Neill, Joe Pearce, Bob Penn, George Rodger, Simon Wide, David Steen, James and Linda Swarbrick and George Whitear. In addition the publishers acknowledge the following photographic agencies for supplying pictures for the book: Camera Press: pages 9, 10, 11 (Loomis Dean), 13, 15 (Herman Leonard), 16 (Simonwide), 20, 23 (Robert Penn), 28, 29 (Terry O'Neill), 14, 15; Rex: 14, 15, 40, 47; Scope: 31, 33; The Kobal Collection: 26, 51; Sygma: 62.

First Carol Publishing Group Edition, 1998

All rights reserved. No part of this book may be reproduced in any form, except by a newspaper or magazine reviewer who wishes to quote brief passages in connection with a review.

A Citadel Press Book
Published by Carol Publishing Group

Citadel Press is a registered trademark of Carol Communications, Inc.

Editorial, sales and distribution, rights and permissions inquiries should be addressed to: Carol Publishing Group, 120 Enterprise Avenue South, Secaucus, NJ 07094

Carol Publishing Group books may be purchased in bulk at special discounts for sales promotion, fund-raising, or educational purposes. Special editions can be created to specifications. For details, contact: Special Sales Department Carol Publishing Group, 120 Enterprise Avenue South, Secaucus, NJ 07094

Published by arrangement with Boxtree an imprint of Macmillan Publishers Ltd London, England

10 9 8 7 6 5 4 3 2 1

ISBN 0-8065-1958-4

Designed by Graham Rye
Printed and bound in Italy by New Interlitho, S.P.A.-Milan

The James Bond Girls deals with the series of James Bond 007 films, from *Dr. No* onwards, made by Eon Productions Ltd. It does not include *Casino Royale* or *Never Say Never Again* which were not made by Eon.

Front cover photographs (left to right): Izabella Scorupco, Barbara Bach, Carey Lowell, Michelle Yeoh, Teri Hatcher, Tanya Roberts, Talisa Soto, Famke Janssen.
© Danjaq Inc and United Artists Corporation. All rights reserved.

Gun symbol logo ©1962 Danjaq LLC and United Artists Corporation. All rights reserved.

Dr. No © 1962 Danjaq LLC and United Artists Corporation. All rights reserved.
From Russia With Love © 1963 Danjaq LLC and United Artists Corporation. All rights reserved.
Goldfinger © 1964 Danjaq LLC and United Artists Corporation. All rights reserved.
Thunderball © 1965 Danjaq LLC and United Artists Corporation. All rights reserved.
You Only Live Twice © 1967 Danjaq LLC and United Artists Corporation. All rights reserved.
On Her Majesty's Secret Service © 1969 Danjaq LLC and United Artists Corporation. All rights reserved.
Diamonds Are Forever © 1971 Danjaq LLC and United Artists Corporation. All rights reserved.
Live And Let Die © 1973 Danjaq LLC and United Artists Corporation. All rights reserved.
The Man With The Golden Gun © 1974 Danjaq LLC and United Artists Corporation. All rights reserved.
The Spy Who Loved Me © 1977 Danjaq LLC and United Artists Corporation. All rights reserved.
Moonraker © 1979 Danjaq LLC and United Artists Corporation. All rights reserved.
For Your Eyes Only © 1981 Danjaq LLC and United Artists Corporation. All rights reserved.
Octopussy © 1983 Danjaq LLC and United Artists Corporation. All rights reserved.
A View To A Kill © 1985 Danjaq LLC and United Artists Corporation. All rights reserved.
The Living Daylights © 1987 Danjaq LLC and United Artists Corporation. All rights reserved.
Licence To Kill © 1989 Danjaq LLC and United Artists Corporation. All rights reserved.
GoldenEye © 1995 Danjaq LLC and United Artists Corporation. All rights reserved.
Tomorrow Never Dies © 1997 Danjaq LLC and United Artists Corporation. All rights reserved.

INTRODUCTION

I often note, with some bemusement, a continuing media usage throughout the world of the phrase 'James Bond Girl' when describing someone of great beauty.

Since Ursula Andress first walked up on that Jamaican beach in *Dr. No* twenty-seven years ago, we have had dozens of ladies in our Bond series. From established actresses to photographic models, in parts large or small, there has been a seemingly never-ending parade of pulchritude in the sixteen productions to date. Whether they were already 'names', or were totally unknown at the time, each and every one of them was given the same appellation by magazines or newspapers . . . a 'James Bond Girl'.

A few have gone on to greater fame, some are still acting with perhaps less success, while many others have retired to marriage, motherhood or business pursuits.

To me, however, every one of them will always be the young and beautiful girl who walked on the set her first day on call.

I am delighted to see so many of them again through this collection of photographs.

Cubby Broccoli

Albert R. Broccoli 1909-1996

James Bond	Sean Connery
Honey Rider	Ursula Andress
Dr. No	Joseph Wiseman
Felix Leiter	Jack Lord
M	Bernard Lee
Miss Taro	Zena Marshall
Sylvia	Eunice Gayson
Miss Moneypenny	Lois Maxwell

Producers .... Harry Saltzman*
.... Albert R. Broccoli*
Director... Terence Young
Screenplay .... Richard Maibaum
.... Johanna Harwood
.... Berkley Mather
Director of Photography .... Ted Moore
Production Designer .... Ken Adam

* The listing as shown is contractual for the Eastern hemisphere and is reversed for the Western hemisphere.

4

The exotic Caribbean island of Jamaica, where Ian Fleming wrote his exciting spy novels, is the picturesque setting for *Dr. No*, the first James Bond film.
After indulging in verbal foreplay with Sylvia Trench at the gaming tables of his London club, James Bond reports to the offices of the British Secret Service. He learns from M that Strangways, their agent in Jamaica, has disappeared along with his secretary. Bond's mission is to investigate their disappearance and discover if it is linked with the 'toppling' of American missiles. Returning to his apartment, Bond is surprised to find Sylvia has gained entry. Dressed only in Bond's pyjama top, high heeled shoes and practising her putting stroke, Sylvia is put off her aim when Bond bursts in, gun in hand. Her face is a picture of disappointment when Bond tells her he must leave immediately. After a kiss he relents, 'almost immediately', he tells her.

No sooner has he landed at Kingston airport than Bond finds that a beautiful female photographer attempts to take his picture and his chauffeur tries to kill him. Suddenly, the exotic island has taken on a more sinister appearance. Bond pays a return visit to Government House and, on leaving the governor's office, catches his secretary, Miss Taro listening at the key hole. Bond decides she bears closer investigation and suggests that she shows him around the island.

After preliminary investigations, Bond discovers the only person who claims to have seen Strangways's new secretary is the suspicious Professor Dent. After finding a receipt from Dent Laboratories at Strangways's bungalow, Bond questions the nervous Professor about the rock samples which the agent had brought to him. Dent says nothing that quells Bond's instinctive doubts about him, so Bond enlists the help of the local fisherman, Quarrel, and CIA agent, Felix Leiter. After checking Quarrel's boat with a Geiger counter, Bond discovers that the rock samples Strangways gathered were radioactive. Either Dent is a bad professor or a poor liar! Bond is determined to find out which.

That evening Bond drives to Miss Taro's bungalow in the mountains for a dinner date. En route he narrowly escapes death at the wheel of his car when a large black hearse attempts to run him off the mountain road. Unfortunately for the 'mourners', they are not so lucky and plummet over the cliff edge to an explosive death. Not surprisingly, Miss Taro is quite speechless at Bond's safe arrival. Telling her, 'Well, you did invite me up here for the view', they retire to the bedroom. After the lovemaking she tells him she will cook dinner at home, in an attempt to keep him at the bungalow. But Bond will have none of it, he is feeling Italian and musical and orders a 'taxi' to take them to a restaurant. On its arrival Miss Taro is decidedly upset when she realizes the 'taxi' holds the local police. 'Book her Superintendent, and mind her nail varnish,' says Bond as he pushes her into the car. She spits in Bond's face.

Bond places the pillows in Taro's bed to give the appearance of a sleeping man, retires to a chair gun in hand, and waits. Some time later a hand appears from behind the bedroom door holding a silenced gun which fires six shots into the 'sleeping figure'. The hand belongs to Professor Dent, and Bond has him at a distinct disadvantage. Dent stalls for time while he clumsily tries to edge his fallen gun nearer. Dent lunges for his gun and fires at Bond, only to hear the hammer fall on an empty magazine. Bond points his Walther PPK menacingly at Dent, 'That was a Smith & Wesson Professor, and you've had your six.' Bond shoots him dead.

Arriving two hours late at Kingston harbour, Bond sets off into the night with Quarrel to investigate the island from which Strangways had collected the radioactive samples – the island of Crab Key, owned by the mysterious Dr. No. Landing safely on the island the two men bed down for the night. Bond is woken from his sleep by the sound of a girl singing 'Underneath the mango tree'. He is treated to the sight of a bikini-clad girl, risen Venus like from the ocean. Bond's appearance from the undergrowth startles her. 'What are you doing here? Looking for shells?' she asks. 'No, I'm just looking,' he replies glibly. Bond learns her name is Honey Rider and that she has been orphaned by Dr. No. She seems carefree and unafraid of discovery by the island's guards as she regularly frequents Crab Key. However, Bond knows it will be different this time.

Bond, Quarrel and Honey successfully evade Dr. No's guards in the mangrove swamps, but after battling with the island's 'dragon' – a diesel-engined swamp

Below left: **Miss Taro was the bait in the trap for 007. Below: Sylvia Trench was adept at indoor games. Right: Honey Rider examines the shells that will fetch her $50 in Miami. Inset: James Bond flirts with Miss Moneypenny.**

vehicle – Quarrel falls victim to its flame-throwing breath, while Bond and Honey are captured by guards wearing protective suits. Bond and Honey are taken to Dr. No's decontamination chamber where they are scrubbed clean to reduce the dangerous radioactive levels their bodies have absorbed in the swamp. Sister Rose and Sister Lily minister to both Bond and Honey's every whim, although Bond's suggestion of two plane tickets to London is politely ignored. After recovering from drugged coffee, Bond and Honey dress for dinner with their gracious host – Dr. No.

Bond and Honey take the elevator into No's underground lair where they are astonished to see a huge glass observation panel with a perfect view of the undersea world. Bond's thoughts are interrupted when a voice from behind interjects, 'One million dollars Mr Bond, you were wondering what it cost. The glass is convex, ten inches thick which accounts for the magnifying effect.' Bond persistently tries to provoke Dr. No. 'Minnows pretending they're whales. Just like you on this island, Dr. No,' retorts Bond. 'It depends Mr Bond, on which side the glass you are,' counters No, winning on points. Over dinner Dr. No explains he works for SPECTRE – Special Executive for Counterintelligence Terrorism Revenge and Extortion. He admits that he thought there might even have been a place for Bond in SPECTRE. Bond tells him he would prefer the revenge department, but of course his first job would be to find the man who killed Strangways and Quarrel. Dr. No is not amused. Telling Bond he is 'just a stupid policeman', No leaves for his control room and orders his guards to soften up his dinner guest.

Bond regains consciousness on the bunk in a prison cell. After negotiating the electrified ventilator grill he finds himself crawling through the air conditioning system. Surviving an attempt to drown him in the tunnelling, Bond makes his way into Dr. No's control room disguised as a technician. During his attempt to destroy the nuclear reactor and abort the Doctor's sabotage of the American missile launch, Bond battles with Dr. No on the descending gantry overlooking the reactor's cooling tank. Bond gains the upper hand and Dr. No is submerged in the now boiling reactor tank when his metal hands are unable to grip the steel legs of the sinking gantry.

Racing from the deserted control room Bond discovers Honey bound hand and foot with water rushing towards her from a sluice gate. Cutting her free, they escape in a small boat just before the reactor reaches critical mass, destroying Dr. No's complex in a shattering explosion. Drifting in their boat after running out of petrol, Bond and Honey are rescued by Felix Leiter and a detachment of marines. However, once taken in tow the castaways decide now is not the time to be rescued and release the tow line during an embrace.

After the runaway success of the first James Bond film this blueprint was adhered to, and is one of the contributing reasons for the longevity of the series.

It was planned that Eunice Gayson (real name Eunice Sargaison) would appear in successive Bond films as 007's home-grown romantic interest Sylvia Trench, and eventually become Mrs Bond. However, she disappeared from the series after *From Russia With Love* (1963). Born in 1931, she trained for the opera, and entered films in 1948, with an appearance in *My Brother Jonathan*. Other roles followed with *Miss Robin Hood* (1952) and *The Revenge of Frankenstein* (1958). She also appeared in many British TV film series and was active in the theatre during the Seventies. She now lives quietly in Surrey, England. Her daughter, Kate, has a small role in *GoldenEye* (1995).

Miss Taro, Dr. No's pawn in the game of kiss n' kill, as portrayed by Zena Marshall was another role in a long line of bad girls and conniving women. She could often be seen in Edgar Wallace thrillers on the arm of a criminal or crooked businessman. Born in Kenya in 1925, she made her stage debut in repertory and first film was *Caesar and Cleopatra* (1945). She also appeared in *The Embezzler* (1954), *The Scarlet Web* (1954), *Those Magnificent Men in their Flying Machines* (1965) and *The Terrornauts* (1967). Now retired, she divides her time between London and the South of France.

The only woman to feature in the life of James Bond as a regular occurrence is of course Miss Moneypenny — portrayed in fourteen of the Bond movies over 23 years by Canadian actress Lois Maxwell (born Lois Hooker in 1927). Her verbal sparring with Connery and Moore was a regular high-point of the series. Starting her career in the same studio stable as Marilyn Monroe, she made her screen debut in *Spring Song* (1946). Lois has appeared in over 50 films and many guest roles in TV series including *The Saint*, *The Avengers* and *Randall and Hopkirk Deceased*. Other appearances include, *The Haunting* (1963), *Operation Kid Brother* (1967) — with Sean Connery's brother Neil — *The Adventurers* (1970) and *Lost and Found* (1979). She wrote a regular column 'Moneypenny' in the *Toronto Sun* for many years and also appeared in a TV commercial for *Brook Street Bureau* as M's famous secretary. Widowed in the 1960s, she has now generally retired from acting and has settled in Frome, Dorset.

Undoubtedly the most memorable of all the Bond girls is Ursula Andress as Honey Rider. The sequence in which she rises from the sea was to secure her screen immortality, and an image by which all subsequent Bond girls would be judged. Born in March 1939 in Bern, Switzerland, Ursula was the daughter of a Swiss diplomat, and showed unusual aptitude in art and chemistry at the Neue Mädchen Schule in Bern. After appearing in many school theatrical productions she was determined to make a career in show business. She found herself in Hollywood at eighteen, where Marlon Brando encouraged her to try acting. Her screen debut came in *The Loves of Casanova* (1954) and subsequent minor roles followed. It was not until her exposure in *Dr. No* (1962) that her face became internationally known. Her most well known appearances include, *Fun in Acapulco* (1964) with Elvis Presley, *She* (1965), *What's New Pussycat?* (1965), the James Bond spoof *Casino Royale* (1967), *Red Sun* (1971) directed by Terence Young, and *Clash of the Titans* (1981). Her private life always seemed to overshadow her career, and she was much in the news when she became a mother at 44 in 1980. She has now generally retired from acting.

5

James Bond	Sean Connery
Tatiana Romanova	Daniela Bianchi
Kerim Bey	Pedro Armendariz
Rosa Klebb	Lotte Lenya
Red Grant	Robert Shaw
M	Bernard Lee
Miss Moneypenny	Lois Maxwell
Major Boothroyd (Q)	Desmond Llewelyn

Producers .... Harry Saltzman
.... Albert R. Broccoli
Director .... Terence Young
Screenplay .... Richard Maibaum
.... Johanna Harwood
Director of Photography .... Ted Moore
Art Director.. Syd Cain

From Russia With Love has James Bond fighting for his life against the machinations of SPECTRE in its attempt to discredit the British Secret Service and gain personal revenge for the death of their operative Dr. No.

After receiving a letter from Tatiana Romanova, a cypher clerk at the Russian consulate in Istanbul, M – head of British Intelligence – summons agent James Bond to his office. The girl wants to defect, and as surety she claims she will bring with her the lektor, a top secret decoding device, but on one condition – that Bond is sent to bring her and the machine back to England. It appears she has fallen in love with the file photo of the British agent. Both Bond and M realize this is a trap, but if there is any chance of them getting a lektor they really must look into it. Before Bond leaves, he is issued with a special black attaché case from Q branch. Major Boothroyd explains to 007 that if he opens the case incorrectly a tear gas cartridge hidden in a magnetised tin of talcum powder will explode – in his face. The case also contains a hidden throwing knife, an AR7 folding sniper's rifle and 50 gold sovereigns – 25 are secreted in each hinge strap. Bond describes this smart-looking piece of luggage as 'a nasty little Christmas present' and doubts he will need it on his mission. It is a rare occasion when agent 007 is proved to be very wrong.

Landing in Istanbul, Bond is driven from the airport to meet Kerim Bey – head of station T Turkey. He is followed by a mysterious black Citroen driven by Russian agents. Kerim tells Bond they must wait for the girl to arrange a meeting. He is followed once more on the journey to his hotel, but the car is now driven by SPECTRE assassin – Red Grant. Bond checks into the hotel, only to discover his room is bugged. Complaining the bed is too small he is given the only room left – the bridal suite. Meanwhile, Grant has left the Russian agent's car parked in front of their consulate – the driver dead on the back seat. The cold war in Istanbul will not remain cold very much longer.

Kerim is 'relaxing' with his girlfriend when a limpet-mine attached to the wall outside explodes, devastating his office. The explosion was timed to catch him at his desk, and he cannot understand why his 'Russian friends' have broken the truce. In an effort to learn the reason behind the attack, Kerim and Bond spy on the consulate from an underground reservoir where Kerim has had a periscope secretly installed. Looking through the eyepiece they discover the perpetrator of the bomb attack was a Bulgarian named Krilencu, whom the Russians use as a killer. 'You should remember him,' says Kerim. 'This man kills for pleasure.'

That evening Kerim takes Bond to an encampment of gipsies, whose 'talents' he uses in a similar fashion to the way the Russians use the Bulgars. Unbeknown to Bond, Kerim and the gipsies, Krilencu and his men are already surrounding the camp. And also lurking in the shadows is Grant. Bond and Kerim have arrived on a bad night. There is to be a fight to the death between Vida and Zora, two gipsy girls who are rivals for the hand in marriage of the chief's son. The girls are led from their caravans and the fight commences. Bond watches, grim faced, as the girls attack each other mercilessly. However, the fight is cut short when shots ring out. Krilencu and his men swarm into the camp shooting at anything that moves. In the foray that follows, Kerim's gun jams and he is injured, and Bond is saved from certain death when Grant shoots an unseen attacker. The Bulgars are beaten off by superior force and Krilencu retreats. Kerim discovers the attack was yet another attempt on his life and he decides to pay Krilencu a final visit with Bond. Kerim and Bond wait in the street outside the killer's hideout. Finally, he is forced to leave through his secret escape exit – a door behind the girl's mouth on a gigantic movie billboard. As Krilencu climbs from his hideout, Kerim shoots him with Bond's sniper rifle and he crashes to the pavement, dead. 'That pays many debts,' sighs Kerim. 'She should have kept her big mouth shut!' suggests Bond.

Bond returns to his hotel exhausted, but soon perks up when he finds Tatiana in

6

his bed wearing nothing but a black choker. 'Guns upset me,' says Tatiana pushing Bond's Walther aside. 'Sorry, I'm a little upset myself,' says Bond. He hopes he will come up to Tania's expectations. 'I will tell you – in the morning,' she promises. Unknown to both Bond and Tania, as she is known to her friends, their bedroom antics are being filmed from behind a large mirror overseen by Rosa Klebb.

After checking the authenticity of the lektor with Tania, Bond and Kerim devise a plan to steal the decoding machine from the consulate. Exploding a smoke bomb underneath the consulate as a diversion, Bond successfully steals the lektor and escapes with Tania and Kerim, to board the Orient Express for the Bulgarian frontier and safety. They are spotted by Russian security man Benz, who leaps aboard as the train moves off. As it leaves the station it is apparent that Grant is also on board. Leaving Kerim with Benz, Bond retires to his compartment to get some sleep. Later, Bond and Tania are about to leave for the restaurant car when the conductor announces, 'There's been a terrible accident!' Both Kerim and Benz are dead in their compartment. Apparently they have killed each other. Hurt and angry at the death of his friend, Bond tries to force Tania to tell him her orders. She says she cannot tell him, 'Even if you kill me, I cannot tell you.' Exasperated, Bond knocks her to the floor. At Belgrade he leaves the train to inform Kerim's son of his father's death, and tells him to arrange via M for someone to meet the train at Zagreb.

Grant intercepts his contact from M at Zagreb and kills him, then re-boards the train posing as the murdered Captain Nash and introduces himself to Bond. When Bond tells Grant he cannot risk taking the lektor through the customs, Grant shows him his planned escape route on a map. As Bond studies the route Grant knocks him unconscious and takes his gun. When Bond has regained his senses, Grant explains how SPECTRE planned to play the British off against the Russians and Bond realizes it was not the Russians' show after all.

Bond opens his briefcase to show Grant it contains gold sovereigns, with which he hopes to bargain for his life, and offers to open Nash's case which should contain more. Bond's haste makes Grant suspicious and he decides to open it himself. As he does, the tear gas cartridge explodes in his face. Bond takes his chance and a vicious fight ensues. Grant almost overpowers Bond, but he takes a knife from the attaché case, and plunges it into Grant's side before strangling him with the wire garrotte from his own wrist watch.

Bond and Tania leave the train, taking the truck that was part of Grant's escape route. They head for a bay where a speedboat is waiting, but en route they are attacked from the air by a SPECTRE helicopter. Bond shoots the co-pilot who then drops a hand grenade inside the cockpit – with explosive results. Thinking they are safe at last, they head for Venice in their speedboat, only to be intercepted by a fleet of SPECTRE gunboats. However, Bond jettisons ruptured fuel drums, igniting them with two well-aimed flares. The SPECTRE fleet is engulfed in flames as Bond quips, 'There's a saying in England – where there's smoke there's fire!'

Now safely in their Venice hotel room, James Bond is making travel arrangements on the telephone when he sees the hotel maid is pointing a gun at him. Too late, he realizes it is Klebb. Klebb is about to pull the trigger when Tania runs back into the room knocking the gun from Klebb's hand. Panic stricken, Klebb lashes out at Bond attempting to kick him with the poisoned blade protruding from the tip of her shoe. As Bond defends himself with a chair Tania shoots Klebb with her own gun. The 'horrible woman' slides down the wall dead. 'She's had her kicks,' Bond says glibly as he takes the gun from Tania's hand. Relaxing in a gondola with Tania, Bond remembers he still has the reel of film that was shot in the bridal suite. Tania asks him what it is. He tells her, 'I'll show you!'

In the series of James Bond movies, *From Russia With Love* is the most faithful to an Ian Fleming novel. Tatiana Romanova is yet another pawn in the villain's master plan.

Runner-up in the 1960 Miss Universe contest and a former Rome fashion model, Daniela Bianchi is a native Italian and after Bond went on to more obscure films like *Weekend Italian Style* (1965), *Dirty Heroes* (1967) and *Operation Kid Brother* (1967) with Sean Connery's brother Neil. She married a Genoan shipping magnate in 1970 by whom she has a son, Fillippo.

Whilst fighting gipsy girl Vida was portrayed by ex-Miss Israel Aliza Gur her opponent was ex-Miss Jamaica Martine Beswick. Martine, now a fabulous-looking 53 year old, first travelled to England at the age of 12 and completed her Grammar school education at 16. She later entered Pitman's College, but left after one term to pursue a career in fashion modelling. In 1960 Martine's family returned to Jamaica. She got a job as an air hostess and did whatever freelance modelling she could. In 1961 she won the title of Miss Jamaica and used the prize money to return to England. She enrolled in a fashion modelling course and was soon working regularly for top publications. Her first contact with the Bond films was when her agent submitted her photos to the producers for the role of the Chinese girl in *Dr. No*. After an interview, it was decided her lack of experience outweighed her good looks, but she was promised a future role if she studied drama – a year later she was given her first dramatic role in *From Russia With Love*. Other roles followed in *The Amorous Adventures of Moll Flanders* (1965) and *The Sandpiper* (1965), until appearing with Bond again in *Thunderball* (1965).

7

Far left: **Tatiana explains she cannot divulge her orders to Bond.**
Left: **Gipsy Vida (Aliza Gur) gains the advantage in her fight with Zora (Martine Beswick). Right: Daniela Bianchi as Russian cypher clerk, Tatiana Romanova. Inset: Bond is 'upset' when he discovers Tania in his bed in the bridal suite.**

JAMES BOND 007
BACK IN ACTION!

ALBERT R. BROCCOLI &
HARRY SALTZMAN PRESENT

SEAN CONNERY

IN IAN FLEMING'S

GOLDFINGER

HONOR BLACKMAN
AS PUSSY GALORE

GERT FROBE
AS GOLDFINGER

TECHNICOLOR®

SCREEN PLAY BY RICHARD MAIBAUM & PAUL DEHN
PRODUCED BY HARRY SALTZMAN & ALBERT R. BROCCOLI
DIRECTED BY GUY HAMILTON   EON PRODUCTIONS LTD

James Bond	**Sean Connery**
Pussy Galore	**Honor Blackman**
Goldfinger	**Gert Frobe**
Jill Masterson	**Shirley Eaton**
Tilly Masterson	**Tania Mallet**
Oddjob	**Harold Sakata**
M	**Bernard Lee**
Felix Leiter	**Cec Linder**
Miss Moneypenny	**Lois Maxwell**
Q	**Desmond Llewelyn**

Producers .... Harry Saltzman
.... Albert R. Broccoli
Director.. Guy Hamilton
Screenplay .... Richard Maibaum
.... Paul Dehn
Production Designer .... Ken Adam
Director of Photography .... Ted Moore

James Bond is pitted against one of his most lethal adversaries, when Auric Goldfinger attempts to break into the world's largest gold depository – Fort Knox.

After escaping the wiles of Latin dancer Bonita and despatching drug smuggler Capungo to a shocking death, James Bond is relaxing at the poolside of the Miami Beach Hotel with Dink, a striking blonde.

Bond is observing the card playing antics of Auric Goldfinger whom he suspects is a cheat. Entering Goldfinger's hotel room, Bond discovers blonde beauty Jill Masterson reclining on the balcony observing Goldfinger's card game through binoculars. By means of a receiver in Goldfinger's hearing-aid she is transmitting the details of his opponent's hand. Bond warns Goldfinger that the Miami Beach

police would not take kindly to what he is doing and tells him to start losing. $15,000 dollars seems a generous amount, says Bond and Goldfinger's face contorts in rage as he snaps his pencil in two. That evening Bond entertains Jill in his hotel bedroom but, while taking a fresh bottle of champagne from the fridge, he is knocked unconscious from behind. Gathering his wits, he is shocked to find Jill is covered from head to toe in gold paint. She has died from skin suffocation. Goldfinger has exacted a terrible revenge.

After receiving a dressing down from M for borrowing Goldfinger's girlfriend, and armed with a bar of gold recovered from a Nazi hoard in Lake Toplitz, Bond arranges an encounter with Goldfinger on the golf course. Goldfinger is neither surprised nor concerned when he meets Bond although, after losing the match to him, he makes it quite clear that further intervention in his affairs would be unwise for 007's health. Goldfinger's Korean manservant Oddjob promptly throws his steel-rimmed bowler hat at a nearby statue, severing its head neatly. Bond comments, 'Remarkable, but what will the Club secretary have to say?' 'Oh, nothing Mr Bond,' says Goldfinger, 'I own the Club.'

Following Goldfinger to Switzerland, Bond encounters a desperate girl in the form of Tilly Soames, but her luggage is initialled T. M. That night Bond stakes out Goldfinger's factory complex. Hearing someone creeping through the undergrowth he discovers it to be Tilly. After wrestling her to the ground she explains that she is Jill Masterson's sister and is determined to avenge her sister's death. Her rifle sets off a trip alarm and Goldfinger's Korean guards, led by Oddjob, are soon on the scene. Tilly runs for the trees as Bond opens fire at the guards from the cover of his Aston Martin DB5. There is a swishing sound followed by a sickening crack as Oddjob's bowler makes contact with Tilly's neck. Bond runs to her fallen body, but it is too late, she is dead. Captured, and with a guard in his car, Bond uses the passenger ejector seat at the first opportunity, and the guard flies out of the car roof. There follows a car chase around Goldfinger's factory, and Bond crashes into a brick wall and falls from the car. As Bond regains consciousness he realizes he is strapped to a table and that Goldfinger is standing over him gloating in triumph as he gives a signal to the control room. The contraption in front of Bond starts to glow and move closer. Goldfinger explains it is an industrial laser which can project a spot on the moon, or at closer range cut through solid metal. He is determined to give Bond a practical demonstration. The laser beam begins to cut through the gold surface of the table, inching ever closer to Bond's groin. Bond admits that Goldfinger has made his point and thanks him for the demonstration. 'Choose your next witticism carefully Mr Bond it maybe your last,' bellows Goldfinger. Bond is desperate, 'Do you expect me to talk?' 'No Mr Bond I expect you to die!' comes the final word from Goldfinger. Only when Bond mentions 'Operation Grand Slam' does he relent to the worried insistence of his Chinese guest, Mr Ling, who has supplied him with the cobalt and iodine atomic device which is to bring a cataclysmic conclusion to Goldfinger's masterplan. Bond is shot with a tranquillizer gun and soon loses consciousness again.

Below left: **The eyes of Latin dance Bonita (Nadja Regin) reflected 007's would-be assassin, Capungo, giving Bond the edge against his brutish opponent. Below: Bond appeals to Pussy's 'maternal' instincts. Right: Honor Blackman as Pussy Galore, judo expert and Goldfinger's personal pilot.**

10

When Bond awakens he is sitting in an aeroplane with a beautiful woman pointing a gun at him. He is not dreaming, the woman is Goldfinger's personal pilot Pussy Galore. They land and Bond is taken to 'Auric Stud' where he is held prisoner. Here he learns the full extent of Goldfinger's plans while hiding under a model of Fort Knox. Goldfinger plans to explode an atomic device in the heart of America's gold reserve making it radioactive for 58 years, thereby increasing the value of his own supply ten times over. Pussy substitutes the deadly nerve gas her pilots are to use in Goldfinger's plan. And Bond is handcuffed to the atomic device and left in the vaults of the Fort Knox bullion depository to die. Meanwhile, outside Fort Knox the 'gassed' American soldiers battle with Goldfinger's Korean troops. Seeing the day is lost Goldfinger escapes, but inside the vault Oddjob battles Bond in a fight to the death. Bond is nearly vanquished by Oddjob's incredible strength, but electrocutes the giant Korean when he tries to retrieve his bowler hat that has become jammed between the bars of the vault room. Bond tries to stop the countdown on the bomb but to no avail. Felix Leiter arrives with a scientist who flicks the right switch in the very nick of time.

His mission accomplished, Bond boards an army plane to visit the President for a personal thank you for saving America's gold reserve but, during the flight, Goldfinger takes over the plane. Bond warns him that it is dangerous to fire guns in aircraft and, distracting his attention, lunges for his gun and the two men wrestle for its possession. The gun goes off, shattering a window and as the cabin depressurizes Goldfinger is sucked through the broken window. Bond struggles to the cabin where Pussy is fighting to gain control of the aircraft. 'Where's Goldfinger?' she asks. 'Playing his golden harp,' replies Bond. The couple parachute to safety, and when a rescue helicopter hovers by Bond pulls Pussy under the 'chute saying, 'Oh no you don't, this is no time to be rescued!'

The women in *Goldfinger* are mainly victims, although Pussy Galore was a reflection of the more liberated and self-sufficient women of the Sixties.

'This kind of exposure is marvellous for my career,' said Shirley Eaton of her role as Jill Masterson in *Goldfinger*. Shirley's gold painted body is probably one of the most enduring images of any Bond film. It even graced the cover of LIFE magazine. The gilding of Shirley had to be done to a strict time limit set by the studio doctors. They warned that after 60 minutes, the continued blocking of the pores by the paint could be dangerous. When the studio make-up man slapped the paint on her 36–22–36 figure, with a doctor and nurse standing by, Shirley gurgled happily. 'It tickles,' she giggled as the brush covered her neck, her back, and even the soles of her feet. A six-inch square on her midriff was left clear of paint as an added precaution – on a doctor's insistence. 'I had flu at the time and it was very uncomfortable – but I felt like a real golden gal,' said Shirley. Her appearance in *Goldfinger* only lasted three minutes, but it is a role that everyone always remembers. After the death of her husband she returned to the UK from the South of France, where they lived together for many years. She abandoned acting in 1969 to devote herself to her family but in more recent years has been trying to make a comeback. Born in 1936, her first film appearance was *You Know What Sailors Are* (1954), and other roles followed in *Around The World Under The Sea* (1965), *The Scorpio Letters* (1966) and *The Seven Men of Sumuru* (1969).

Tania Mallet abandoned modelling to co-star in *Goldfinger* as Tilly Masterson. She didn't take to acting and subsequent offers were met with a blank refusal. She married twice, inheriting three step-children with her second husband, a toy manufacturer. She enjoys gardening. *Goldfinger* was her only screen role.

Born in 1925, Honor Blackman's wartime career as a Home Office despatch rider seemed to brand her as the adventurous type but, having enrolled in the Rank Charm School, it was decided to cast her as an English Rose. It was not until many years later that she was able to break her screen image with the portrayal of Pussy Galore. 'Before Bond, the parts I used to play in films were demure, sweet, antiseptic and antisex,' she said. 'I wasn't even allowed to think like a woman. Pussy Galore and 007 worked wonders for me.' It was unnecessary for her to test for the role as the film-makers already knew what she could do from her appearances in TV's *The Avengers*. At the time of the film's release, there was an uproar over the name Pussy Galore and the film-makers were unable to get it past the American censors. Then *Goldfinger* opened in London and Honor was presented to Prince Philip. The next day the newspapers ran a picture of them headlined 'Pussy and the Prince'. That was the clincher. The American censor gave the film the all-clear. Honor's career has been consistently successful on stage, screen and TV, notably during the 90s in *The Upper Hand*. Other films include *Jason and the Argonauts* (1963), *A Twist of Sand* (1967), *Shalako* (1968) with Sean Connery, and *The Cat and The Canary* (1976).

Two of the smaller roles in *Goldfinger* warrant mention here. Nadja Regin, the Latin night club dancer Bonita is one of the few actresses who holds the distinction of appearing in two Bond movies, the other being *From Russia With Love* (1963) in which she played Kerim Bey's girlfriend; while Margaret Nolan as Dink shared a poolside scene with Sean Connery and is also the 'golden girl' featured in Robert Brownjohn's opening and closing credit titles for *Goldfinger*.

Left: **Shirley Eaton with the golden look that brought her international fame. Inset: Shirley's gilding had to be done to a strict time limit. Right: Seeking to avenge the death of her sister, Tilly Masterson takes aim at Goldfinger. Below: Shirley Eaton as Jill Masterson. Below right: Bond relaxes in Miami with the ample Dink.**

James Bond	Sean Connery
Domino	Claudine Auger
Largo	Adolfo Celi
Fiona	Luciana Paluzzi
Felix Leiter	Rik Van Nutter
M	Bernard Lee
Miss Moneypenny	Lois Maxwell
Q	Desmond Llewelyn

Presented by .... Harry Saltzman
.... Albert R. Broccoli
Producer.. Kevin McClory
Director.. Terence Young
Screenplay .... Richard Maibaum
.... John Hopkins
Based on the original story by .... Ian Fleming,
.... Kevin McClory and Jack Whittingham
Production Designer .... Ken Adam
Director of Photography .... Ted Moore

12

Thunderball takes James Bond to the Bahamas in search of a hijacked Vulcan bomber and its deadly cargo of nuclear bombs stolen by the criminal organization SPECTRE. After despatching an old enemy in France with the aid of Sûreté agent Mademoiselle La Porte, Bond takes a rest cure at the health farm Shrublands. Here he becomes involved with his physiotherapist Patricia Fearing and survives an attempt on his life by SPECTRE agent Count Lippe. On leaving the health farm in his specially equipped Aston Martin DB5, Bond is followed by Lippe who opens fire on him with a revolver. Before Bond is able to use the Aston's special armaments, a speeding motorbike fires two deadly rockets at Lippe's car sending it crashing off the road where it explodes in a ball of flame. Bond is to meet the motorcyclist later – but in very different circumstances.

When Bond reports to M that he has seen the pilot of the missing Vulcan bomber dead at the health farm it prompts the Secret Service chief to assign him to Nassau, where the pilot's sister Domino is living. Bond arrives in the Bahamas and teams up with the Service's local agent Paula Catlin and CIA agent Felix Leiter. Bond makes initial contact with Domino when he admires her form underwater. Later, when he meets her at the casino, he learns she is the mistress of Emilio Largo, whose yacht, the Disco Volante is suspected of carrying the stolen atom bombs. The following night Bond inspects the hull of the Disco Volante underwater and is attacked by a frogman sentry. The alarm raised, Bond is pursued by Largo's men who proceed to throw grenades into the water in order to depth-charge the unknown intruder. Faking his death, Bond eludes Largo's men and swims to shore. A speeding car stops to give him a lift. The driver is SPECTRE agent Fiona Volpe – the motorcyclist who despatched Lippe in England. Bond notices she is wearing a large ring identical to one worn by Largo. Coincidentally, Fiona happens to be staying at the same hotel as Bond.

Bond investigates Largo's home Palmyra when Leiter reports that Paula is missing. Bond discovers her dead by her own hand in the basement of Largo's island headquarters. She has taken cyanide rather than suffer at the hands of her captors.

Bond barely escapes with his life when he has an exceedingly close encounter in the shark pool. Once back at his hotel, Bond discovers Fiona has now been moved into Paula's room. When Bond finds Fiona in the bath she asks him to hand her something to put on. Bond, ever the gentleman, hands her her slippers! They retire to the bedroom, and after the lovemaking, Fiona shows her true colours when Bond is taken prisoner by Largo's henchmen – but not before Fiona has made her feelings about Bond quite clear. 'James Bond, who only has to make love to a woman and she starts to hear heavenly choirs singing. She repents and immediately returns to the side of right and virtue – but not this one! What a blow it must have been, *you* having a failure.' Bond's comment – 'Well, you can't win them all!'

Bond escapes from his captors and is chased through the Junkanoo carnival. Fiona catches up with him at the Kiss Kiss Club, where on the dance floor she steers him towards the waiting gun of her henchman. At the last moment Bond spins round, and the bullet meant for him hits Fiona in the back and kills her instantly. Bond leaves her body seated at one of the club tables, asking a couple dining, 'Do you mind if my friend sits this one out – she's just dead!'

Bond and Domino visit Love Beach where he tells her of the death of her brother. Domino asks Bond to promise that he will kill Largo for her. Their conversation is overheard by Vargas, Largo's henchman, who has followed them. Domino warns Bond as Vargas levels his pistol ready for the kill. Bond turns unexpectedly, firing his spear-gun, which pins Vargas to a palm tree – 'I think he got the point!'

After escaping from an underwater cavern where he had been stranded by Largo, Bond leads the American aqua-troopers against the SPECTRE chief and his force

Below left & right: **Molly Peters as 'physical therapist' Patricia Fearing administers a little TLC – 'Tender Loving Care' – to James Bond during his stay at Shrublands health farm. Right: Domino Derval, the 'plaything' of SPECTRE number two, Emilio Largo.**

14

of frogmen in a fierce and bloody underwater battle. Largo escapes aboard the Disco Volante as his men are overcome by the superior American forces, aided by Bond wearing his underwater jet-pack. Climbing aboard the speeding hydrofoil Bond battles with Largo and his cabin crew. He is knocked senseless to the floor, and Largo is about to shoot him when Domino appears from below deck and fires a harpoon into the SPECTRE chief's back. Largo slumps dead over the hydrofoil's controls. 'I'm glad he's dead,' says Domino. 'You're glad!' retorts Bond. Realizing the SPECTRE chief has jammed the controls of the hydrofoil, Bond and Domino leap into the relative safety of the sea as the Disco Volante runs aground on the rocks, exploding on impact. Sitting in a rubber dinghy, a puzzled Domino watches as Bond inflates a large red balloon tied to a rope which he clips to his diving suit. The balloon floats into the air where an American Air Force plane catches the rope and whisks Bond and Domino into the air – and safety.

The women in *Thunderball* are more assertive than in the previous three films, although Bond is still allowed the obligatory 'plaything'.

Molly Peters who portrayed the 'physical' therapist Patricia Fearing hails from Walsham-le-Willows in Suffolk, England and was a brunette prior to her role in *Thunderball*. She left her parents' farm in 1960 to come to London where she started work as a shop girl. Many of Molly's London friends thought her 37-24-37 figure would secure her future as a glamour model, and taking their advice she became a pin-up and nude photo-model. It was while she was one of a crowd of extras in a scene for *The Amorous Adventures of Moll Flanders* (1965) that she was spotted by the film's director Terence Young. After she had appeared in her second film, *Joey Boy* (1965), Young, the director of *Thunderball*, suggested that she audition for the role of Patricia. Molly was the first nude – albeit in silhouette behind frosted glass – to appear in a Bond film. She has now retired from acting and lives with her husband in Suffolk.

Fiona Volpe, the readheaded SPECTRE killer was one of the most memorable female roles in the entire series. This girl meant to kill Bond — and anyone else who stood her way! Portrayed by Italian actress Luciana Paluzzi, this was a bad girl who enjoyed being bad! Among her many film and TV roles Luciana also appeared in *The Man From U.N.C.L.E.* film *To Trap A Spy* (1965), in which she also tried to kill Napoleon Solo. She has also appeared in *Chuka* (1967), *The Amazons* (1973), and *The Cop That Loved Me* (1978). Now a successful businesswoman she is married to an American TV millionaire, and has one son.

Martine Beswick who portrayed Bond's Bahamian assistant Paula Catlin was the first girl to hold the distinction of appearing in two Bond films as different characters — and be involved with 007 on both occasions. Her first Bond appearance was in *From Russia With Love* (1963) as the fighting gipsy girl Zora. Martine has also appeared in *One Million Years BC* (1966), *Slave Girls* (1967), *Dr.Jekyll and Sister Hyde* (1971) and *The Happy Hooker Goes To Hollywood* (1980). She has also made numerous appearances in TV features such as *Falcon Crest* (1985).

Domino, the pawn in Largo's game of nuclear blackmail was portrayed as a vulnerable plaything by Claudine Auger. Her 5ft 8in 37-25-37 figure helped win her the title of Miss France at the tender age of 15. She later came to England where she was an au pair for a London family. The film-makers eventually chose Claudine from a short list of four actresses who had been drawn from 600 possible girls — one of whom had been Raquel Welch. When Claudine's family heard of her winning the role it was her sister Anne-Marie who was most impressed, her bedroom was plastered with pictures of her favourite star — Sean Connery! Claudine is still friendly with Connery who, she says, 'was just like a big brother to me' during filming. Her first screen appearance was in *Le Testament d'Orphée* in 1959. She has also appeared in *Triple Cross* (1966), *The Crimebuster* (1977) and *The Associate* (1982), and in advertisements for the French Concorde. She has now generally retired from acting, although did appear in the Granada TV series *The Memoirs of Sherlock Holmes* (1993). Claudine is married to a British-based businessman and commutes regularly between London and Paris.

Left & below: **Whether astride a rocket-firing motorbike or dressed for the beach, Fiona Volpe was just as deadly.** Top left: **Paula Catlin (Martine Beswick), 007's assistant in Nassau.** Right & top far right: **Domino suffered torture at the hands of Largo before exacting her revenge with a well-aimed speargun.** Centre far right: **Bond with Sûreté agent Mlle La Porte (Mitsouko) and** (below) **in an off-duty moment.**

James Bond	Sean Connery
Aki	Akiko Wakabayashi
Kissy	Mie Hama
Tiger Tanaka	Tetsuro Tamba
Mr Osato	Teru Shimada
Helga Brandt	Karin Dor
Blofeld	Donald Pleasence
M	Bernard Lee
Miss Moneypenny	Lois Maxwell
Q	Desmond Llewelyn

Producers .... Harry Saltzman
.... Albert R. Broccoli
Director... Lewis Gilbert
Screenplay .... Roald Dahl
Production Designer .... Ken Adam
Director of Photography .... Freddie Young

James Bond travels to Japan to combat SPECTRE's plot to start World War III from their base inside a hollow volcano.

James Bond reports to M on board a nuclear submarine, fresh from his own 'funeral' at sea. 'Now that you're dead perhaps some of your old friends will leave you alone,' says M.

An American space capsule has been hijacked by an intruder spacecraft and the Americans suspect the Russians. World peace is balanced on a knife edge, and Bond has to work fast to discover the base of the renegade spacecraft as another American launch is imminent.

Once on the Japanese mainland Bond is contacted by Aki at a Sumo hall and is driven to meet his contact Henderson in Tokyo. Henderson, however, is murdered before he can finish briefing the British agent, but Bond crashes through the paper wall and catches the assassin, killing him with his own knife. Seeing the assassin's driver waiting for his return, Bond disguises himself in the dead man's clothes and crawls into the back seat of the car feigning injury. The driver takes him to a large modern building, the offices of Osato Chemicals. Carrying Bond on his shoulder, the driver enters an office and places the impostor on a couch. 'Good evening' smiles Bond, quickly drawing his gun, but the driver is quicker, and throws Bond through the paper walls. Bond fights for his life as he is thrown all over the office, and threatened with decapitation with a Samurai sword. Bond eventually finishes the bout by smashing the driver over the head with a large stone statuette. Bond notices that a panel covering the safe door is open and decides to investigate. Using an automatic safe-cracking device, Bond successfully opens the safe but sets off an alarm in the process. Grabbing a handful of documents he escapes from the pursuing guards with the help of Aki in her Toyota sports car.

Bond wants some answers, but before he can get Aki to talk he has to catch her. She runs into the deserted subway until Bond catches up with her, but then mysteriously stands her ground. As Bond walks towards her the ground opens up beneath his feet and he finds himself hurtling down a metal chute. He is dumped unceremoniously in an armchair at the end of the chute. 'Welcome Bond-san. I am so very pleased to meet you.' Bond has stumbled into the secret underground office of Tiger Tanaka – head of the Japanese Secret Service – and Aki is his top agent. When examining the documents stolen from Osato's safe they find a link with the ship *Ning-Po*. Bond retires with Tiger to his house, where he receives his first 'civilized' bath.

The next day Bond returns to Osato's office posing as Mr Fisher, the managing director of Empire Chemicals. Bond is introduced to Osato's confidential secretary Helga Brandt, and it is quite apparent that he is recognized as the intruder of the previous night. Osato gives the order to kill Bond and as 007 leaves the building he is shadowed by a car full of gunmen who open fire on him. Once again Aki rushes to the rescue in her sports car and the gunmen follow in hot pursuit. Aki radios Tiger asking for the 'usual reception' for the gunmen, and suddenly, a helicopter swoops down and lifts the attackers' car into the air on the end of a large magnet then promptly drops them in Tokyo Bay. 'Just a drop in the ocean,' says Bond.

Aki and Bond drive to Kobe docks where the *Ning-Po* is berthed and where they are promptly attacked by dock workers in Osato's pay. Bond tells Aki to escape while he fights off their pursuers. After eluding his attackers, Bond is suddenly knocked out from behind. On regaining consciousness, he finds himself tied to a chair aboard the *Ning-Po* with Helga Brandt threatening him with a scalpel. He convinces her that he is an industrial spy and they can share the profit of his night raid on Osato's safe. She cuts him free, and he returns the favour by cutting the straps on her dress saying, 'Oh the things I do for England!' Helga pretends that she will fly him to Tokyo, but bails out of the plane leaving Bond to his fate. Luckily, 007 is able to land the aircraft before it explodes in a mass of flame.

> Below left: **Moneypenny aboard M's submarine headquarters.** Below: **Bond and Kissy relax during their ascent of the volcano.** Right: **Kissy Suzuki in her ceremonial wedding costume.**

Bond rejoins Tiger and Aki and learns that they have discovered the island destination of the *Ning-Po*. The autogyro, *Little Nellie*, has arrived along with her father. 'Welcome to Japan Dad' Bond tells Q, who isn't impressed with 007's juvenile quips. 'I have much curiosity Bond-san,' says a very puzzled Tanaka, 'What is *Little Nellie*?' 'Oh she's very small, quite fast, she can do anything. Quite your type really,' says Bond. 007 takes to the skies over the island in the autogyro, and while investigating the volcanoes discovers that he has company in the form of four SPECTRE helicopters. Using his flying arsenal he successfully destroys the enemy aircraft and flys to meet Tiger at the Ninja training school. During the night a SPECTRE assassin kills Aki when posion meant for Bond drips onto her lips. Bond shoots the attacker dead, but he is too late to save Aki. Bond is then transformed into a Japanese by Tiger's bath girls in readiness for his trip to the Ama island.

Meanwhile, inside SPECTRE's headquarters, Blofeld summons Osato and Helga Brandt before him. They have allowed James Bond to escape and someone must pay. Blofeld presses a foot pedal under his desk and Helga falls to her doom, to be consumed by a shoal of voracious piranhas.

Bond is 'married' to Tiger's agent Kissy Suzuki, and they travel to the Ama diving island of Matsu. That night Bond and Kissy are awoken with Tiger's news that the Americans have brought their launch date forward to midnight.

Investigating a grotto where a diving girl had recently been found dead, Bond and Kissy are forced to swim for their lives when Bond realizes the cavern is full of poison gas. Making their way to the top of the volcano, they are puzzled to see a helicopter descending into its crater. Reaching the edge of the crater, Bond tests the depth of the lake, only to find it is made of metal. As Bond begins to walk across the false lake the surface starts to slide back to reveal SPECTRE's headquarters. Kissy makes her way back down the volcano to fetch Tiger and his Ninjas, while Bond enters the headquarters with the aid of rubber suction cups strapped to his hands and knees. Attempting to take the place of a SPECTRE astronaut, Bond is captured and brought before Blofeld.

'They told me you were assassinated in Hong Kong,' Blofeld says smugly. 'Yes. This is my second life,' retorts Bond, looking death in the face. 'You only live twice Mr Bond,' says Blofeld with an eerie ring of finality.

Tiger and his Ninjas appear in the crater just after the blast off of the intruder rocket and are met with a hail of automatic gunfire. Bond manages to open the crater roof for a short time to give the Ninjas a fighting chance. One Ninja manages to attach a limpet mine to the crater ceiling which blows a gaping hole in the roof. The remainder of Tiger's force then absail into the volcano, where they engage SPECTRE's forces in a final battle. Blofeld escapes from the control room taking Bond and Osato with him. After shooting Osato, Blofeld takes aim at Bond, but a well-aimed Ninja throwing star from Tiger finds its mark, and the wounded Blofeld escapes in his monorail. Bond has to get to the exploder button in the control room to destroy the intruder spacecraft, but first he must get past Hans, Blofeld's massive bodyguard. Hans delivers a crashing blow to Bond's face, but without serious damage and eventually Bond despatches him into the ever hungry jaws of the piranhas. Racing into the blazing control room Bond destroys the intruder spacecraft and averts World War III. Meanwhile, Blofeld sets off an explosive chain reaction in order to destroy his base with the intruders inside. Bond, Kissy, Tiger and the surviving Ninjas run for their lives with the volcano exploding around them. Swimming out to sea, Bond and Kissy clamber into a rubber dinghy as Blofeld's headquarters disappear in a volcanic eruption. As Bond embraces Kissy, M's submarine emerges from the sea under their dinghy.

Born in Tokyo on 20 November 1943, Mie Hama started earning her living as a bus conductress at the age of 16. She was considered tall by Japanese standards at 5 ft 4½ ins and had been a contract artist at Toho Studios since she was 17. The most photographed girl in her country, she was often described as the Japanese Brigitte Bardot. Her 35–23–35 figure graced countless homespun movies before appearing as Kissy Suzuki. She continues to appear in TV and films in Japan.

Another contract player at Toho Studios, Akiko Wakabayashi had played policewomen, secret agents and spies in countless Japanese films prior to her role as Aki. Half an inch shorter than her colleague, Akiko's 35–23–35½ figure was also seen in the Italian film *Le Orientale* (1959) playing a diving girl, and in the German production *Haruka Naru Neppu*.

Osato's confidential secretary, Karin Dor, added another role to her long line of character parts. Born in Wiesbaden, Germany, she made her debut at 16 in *The Silent Angel* opposite Christine Kaufmann. She was known as 'Miss Crime' in her homeland because of the countless gangster films in which she appeared – although always as the good girl. A busy and much travelled actress she has worked in Germany, Italy, Spain and Yugoslavia. She also appeared in *The Face of Fu Manchu* (1965) opposite Christopher Lee and *Topaz* (1969).

19

Opposite: **Bad girl, Helga Brandt.** Below left: **Aki helps 007 relax, Japanese style.** Below top: **Bond and Kissy are due to be interrupted by M's submarine.** Below bottom: **007 has his first 'civilized' bath.**

FAR UP! FAR OUT! FAR MORE!
James Bond 007 is back!

HARRY SALTZMAN and ALBERT R. BROCCOLI present
JAMES BOND 007 in IAN FLEMING'S
"ON HER MAJESTY'S SECRET SERVICE"

starring GEORGE LAZENBY · DIANA RIGG · TELLY SAVALAS as Blofeld

also starring GABRIELE FERZETTI and ILSE STEPPAT

Produced by HARRY SALTZMAN and ALBERT R. BROCCOLI
Directed by PETER HUNT · Screenplay by RICHARD MAIBAUM
Music by JOHN BARRY · PANAVISION® · TECHNICOLOR®
Original motion picture soundtrack available on United Artists Records

James Bond	George Lazenby
Tracy	Diana Rigg
Blofeld	Telly Savalas
Draco	Gabriele Ferzetti
Irma Bunt	Ilse Steppat
Sir Hilary Bray	George Baker
M	Bernard Lee
Miss Moneypenny	Lois Maxwell
Q	Desmond Llewelyn

Producers	Harry Saltzman
	Albert R. Broccoli
Director	Peter Hunt
Screenplay	Richard Maibaum
Director of Photography	Michael Reed
Production Designer	Syd Cain

The world food supply is under threat from bacteriological sabotage and James Bond is once more on the trail of Ernst Stavro Blofeld.

Driving along a coastal road in Portugal, James Bond is overtaken at speed by a car driven by a beautiful woman. Driving further down the coast he notices the same woman walking fully clothed into the sea. Realizing that she is attempting suicide, Bond races to the sea's edge and plucks her from a watery grave. Lifting her onto the sand, he is surprised by two men. The woman is dragged back to her car while Bond is ordered to lie down in a fishing boat. As one man levels his gun to shoot, Bond throws a grappling hook from the boat at him and a vicious fight ensues in the surf and on the beach. Having dealt with both men, Bond is left holding the woman's shoes as she races off in her car. Bond checks into his hotel

and is surprised to find that the woman from the beach is also staying there. After paying her gambling debt at the casino, he discovers that she is the Comtessa Teresa di Vicenzo – but her friends call her Tracy. She invites Bond to her room, but on entering he is surprised by a powerful black assailant whom he knocks cold. Returning to his own room, Bond finds Tracy ready to repay her debt. After a night of lovemaking Bond wakes to find that Tracy has gone. She has left a rose and some gambling chips on the pillow – he has been paid in full.

Leaving the hotel for a game of golf Bond is intercepted by the men he fought on the beach and taken to a demolition yard where he meets Marc Ange Draco, Tracy's father and head of a Mafia-type organization, the Union Corse. Draco explains to Bond that Tracy has been an awkward and unhappy child since the death of her mother, and that he fears for her life due to her fragile mental state. He feels Bond is the kind of man who could give her the stability she desperately needs, and offers him a million pounds if he will marry her. Bond tells Draco he doesn't need the money and, apart from that, a wife would be a liability for a man in his profession. Draco tempts Bond with information about the whereabouts of Blofeld, telling him he wouldn't tell Her Majesty's Secret Service, but he would tell his future son-in-law. Bond agrees to go along to Draco's birthday celebrations which Tracy always attends. Realizing that Bond has only attended the party to gather information, Tracy forces her father to tell Bond what he wants to know. She runs off feeling she has been used yet again, but Bond goes after her, and a real bond of affection is formed between them in the following weeks.

Armed with the knowledge that Blofeld has been dealing with a lawyer in Berne called Gumbold, Bond leaves for Switzerland. He discovers that Blofeld has been using Gumbold as a go-between with the Royal College of Arms in London in his attempt to establish his right to the title of Count de Bleuchamp. He is expecting a visit from one Sir Hilary Bray on the matter.

With the cooperation of the College of Arms, Bond impersonates Sir Hilary and travels to Blofeld's mountain top hideaway – Piz Gloria. Bond is introduced to Blofeld and is accepted as the representative of the College. However, when he is caught seducing several of the beautiful girls at Blofeld's Institute of Physiological Research, including Ruby and Nancy, he is exposed as agent 007. Blofeld explains that the girls are his angels of death, and that once returned to their own countries they will administer deadly bacteria into the food chain by a secret method. Bond asks Blofeld how many millions he plans to extort this time, and is amused to find that Blofeld's request is for little more than recognition to the title of Count and amnesty for his past crimes.

Bond later discovers the manner in which the angels of death are to administer their deadly bacteria. While under hypnosis, the girls have been given their instructions as well as a compact and atomizer as a going-away Christmas present. The gifts contain a receiver and the bacteria. Blofeld will trigger the girls simultaneously to administer the virus. Knowing he must get this information urgently to London, Bond steals some skis and escapes down the mountainside

Below left: **Angela Scoular as Ruby.** Below: **Bond encounters Tracy at her father's birthday celebration.** Right: **Diana Rigg as Tracy – the only woman to become Mrs James Bond.**

with, hot on his heels, Blofeld's pursuing guards. Managing to reach a small town in the valley, Bond is pleasantly surprised to find Tracy has followed him there. She helps him escape from his pursuers, and running into a snowstorm, they seek refuge for the night in a barn. The next morning Blofeld and his guards reach the barn, but too late. When Blofeld spots them skiing down the mountain he sends his guards to head them off at the precipice. Bond manages to escape but Blofeld causes a tremendous avalanche which engulfs Tracy. Blofeld's men drag Tracy from the snow.

M refuses to help rescue Tracy and Bond telephones Draco to ask him if he is interested in a demolition job. Flying out of the alpine dawn in helicopters, Bond and Draco attack Blofeld's headquarters in force. Inside Tracy fights for her life against Blofeld's henchmen, despatching one with a champagne bottle and impaling the other on a set of ornamental spikes. Bond rushes into the laboratory looking for Blofeld, while Draco's men set explosive charges to destroy the complex. Tracy, who does not want to leave without Bond, is manhandled into a helicopter by her father. Still searching for Blofeld, Bond is surprised from behind when the SPECTRE chief opens fire on him with a machine-gun. Both Blofeld and Bond leap from the building as the explosive charges destroy the institute forever. Chasing Blofeld down a toboggan run, Bond is blown off course by a hand grenade thrown at him by the fleeing man. Managing to leap onto Blofeld's toboggan, Bond struggles furiously with him until the SPECTRE chief becomes caught in the low hanging bough of a tree.

James Bond is reunited with Tracy at her father's ranch in Portugal – it is their wedding day! M, Moneypenny and Q are all in attendance to wish the happy couple good luck. Q hasn't always seen eye to eye with 007 but says, 'If there's anything you ever need.' 'Thank you Q,' replies Bond, 'but this time I've got the gadgets, and I know how to use them.'

Mr and Mrs Bond leave for their honeymoon in their flower adorned Aston Martin. A little way into their journey Bond stops on a mountain road to remove the flowers. Suddenly without warning machine-gun fire from a passing Mercedes strafes their car. 'It's Blofeld,' shouts Bond leaping into the car. Only then does Bond realize that Tracy is dead.

He cradles her softly in his arms weeping, 'We have all the time in the world.'

The film follows Fleming's writing very closely and in essence the women in the film are characters in his novel.

With the casting of an inexperienced actor in the role of James Bond, it was important that the leading lady was a seasoned actress, and Diana Rigg was certainly a good choice. Her portrayal of Tracy as Bond's equal brought a freshness and vitality to the part, and it is probably her best screen performance. Diana came to Bond fresh from TV's *The Avengers* and this is reflected in her fight scenes in *On Her Majesty's Secret Service*. Other appearances include, *The Assassination Bureau* (1968) with Oliver Reed, *The Hospital* (1971) with George C. Scott and *Theatre of Blood* (1973) with Vincent Price. Her first love is the theatre, where she has achieved considerable success in such roles as Heloise in *Abelard and Heloise* (1970), *Lady Macbeth* (1971), Eliza Doolittle in *Pygmalion* (1974) and more recently in Stephen Sondheim's *Follies* and the Greek tragedy *Medea*. She was awarded the title of Dame in 1994.

Angela Scoular appeared as Bond's bedtime partner Ruby. She has appeared in TV productions such as *Penmarric*, and her varied stage roles have included Ophelia to Alan Bates's *Hamlet*. Her films include, *Casino Royale* (1967), *Here We Go Round the Mulberry Bush* (1967) and *Great Catherine* (1968). She is married to the actor Leslie Phillips.

Catherine Von Schell played Nancy, Bond's other bedmate at Piz Gloria who beat Blofeld's curfew to get her man. Her other appearances include *Moon Zero Two* (1969) and TV's *Space 1999*.

'Of course I know what he's allergic to!' is the bitchy line delivered by Joanna Lumley when Bond masquerades as Sir Hilary Bray. Joanna found success in TV's *Avengers* after her appearance with Bond and earlier TV successes have been followed by the acclaimed comedy series *Absolutely Fabulous*. In 1995, she was awarded the OBE.

Far left: **'We have all the time in the world'** – the happiness of Bond's and Tracy's wedding day is soon to be shattered by tragedy. Left: **Bond is surrounded by Blofeld's 'Angels of Death'** – whom he has brainwashed into infecting the world's food supply (back row) **Julie Ege, Anoushka Hempel, Dani Sheridan, Jenny Hanley, Catherine von Schell,** (front row) **Mona Chong, Zara, Ingrid Black** (foreground) **Joanna Lumley.** Below: **Joanna Lumley in an early screen role.**

James Bond	Sean Connery
Tiffany Case	Jill St. John
Blofeld	Charles Gray
Plenty O'Toole	Lana Wood
Willard Whyte	Jimmy Dean
Saxby	Bruce Cabot
Mr Kidd	Putter Smith
Mr Wint	Bruce Glover
Leiter	Norman Burton
M	Bernard Lee
Q	Desmond Llewelyn
Miss Moneypenny	Lois Maxwell

Producers .... Harry Saltzman
.... Albert R. Broccoli
Director.. Guy Hamilton
Screenplay .... Richard Maibaum
.... Tom Mankiewicz
Director of Photography .... Ted Moore
Production Designer .... Ken Adam

James Bond battles again with Blofeld – and his doubles – when he holds the world to ransom with a laser orbiting in space.

Discovering Blofeld's whereabouts, Bond infiltrates his headquarters and, after disposing of his bodyguards, dispatches him smartly to his death in a pool of boiling mud. 'Welcome to hell Blofeld,' says Bond as the SPECTRE chief's body sinks below the surface.

With the death of 'Blofeld', Bond is able to concentrate on his next mission. Visiting the London headquarters of a diamond syndicate, Bond and M learn from Sir Donald Munger that a large number of diamonds are going missing from a South African mining operation. Unusually, the diamonds are not turning up on the black market. Someone is stockpiling them, and Bond is given the job of discovering who is organizing the smuggling pipeline and why.

Assuming the identity of professional smuggler Peter Franks, Bond travels to Amsterdam and makes contact with Tiffany Case, the next link in the chain. Bond learns that Tiffany was named after the famous store in New York where her mother gave birth to her while shopping for a wedding ring. 'Well I'm glad for your sake it wasn't Van Cleef and Arpels,' remarks Bond. Back at his hotel Bond learns from Q that the real Peter Franks has killed his guard and escaped. Rushing back to Tiffany's apartment, Bond intercepts Franks at the front door of the building. Moving into the elevator Bond tries to overpower him and a fierce struggle ensues. Arriving at Tiffany's floor, Bond and Franks fall from the elevator knocking a fire extinguisher from the wall. Bond grabs the extinguisher, sprays it in Franks's face and knocks him into the stair well to his death. Switching wallets with the dead man, Bond drags the corpse into Tiffany's apartment where she searches the body for identification. 'Oh my god you've just killed James Bond,' squeals Tiffany brandishing Bond's Playboy Club-card. 'Is that who it was?' says Bond feigning indifference. 'Well, it just proves no one is indestructible.'

Hiding the diamonds in Franks's body, Bond and Tiffany fly to Las Vegas where Bond is collected by a hearse full of gangsters. Posing as Franks's brother, Bond is driven to Slumber Incorporated funeral home where the diamonds are separated from the body during its cremation. Bond is knocked unconscious by gay killers Wint and Kidd, and placed in a coffin which they send into the flames of the crematorium. But when the diamonds are discovered to be fake, Morton Slumber opens the coffin and demands to know what Bond has done with the real gems. Bond climbs out of the still smoking coffin and heads for the Tropicana Hotel, where he later visits the casino. 'Hi there I'm Plenty, Plenty O'Toole,' comes a voice from Bond's side at the crap table. 'Named after your father perhaps,' replies Bond viewing the girl's obvious charms. Collecting their winnings, Plenty and Bond retire to his room but are interrupted by three gunmen who proceed to throw Plenty out of the window. 'Exceptionally fine shot,' says Bond as Plenty lands safely in a swimming pool ten floors below. 'I didn't know there was a pool down there,' replies the gunman as Bond knocks him to the floor. To Bond's astonishment the gunmen retreat dragging their unconscious colleague with them. Bond then realizes that Tiffany is waiting for him in the bedroom.

The next morning Bond and Felix Leiter's men are given the slip by Tiffany when she disappears with the real gems. Bond goes to Tiffany's house where he finds Plenty dead in the swimming pool. Bond forces Tiffany to tell him where she has left the diamonds. Establishing the gems are now in the possession of Dr. Metz, Bond and Tiffany follow him to Willard Whyte's Techtronics Factory. Once inside, Bond observes Metz's technicians constructing a curious-looking machine. Bond is soon recognized as an intruder, and he clambers over an artificial moonscape to escape in a nearby moon-buggy. Bond and Tiffany return to the streets of Las Vegas only to be chased by the local police force. Bond resourcefully escapes by taking his car up on two wheels and down a narrow alleyway.

After resting with Tiffany on a water bed filled with fish, Bond decides to visit the mysterious millionaire, Willard Whyte. Climbing from the window he hitches a ride on top of the outside of the elevator, which takes him to Whyte's penthouse suite. After mountaineering on the outside of the building, Bond finally gains entry

---

Below: **Bond encounters opposition from Bambi (Trina Parks) and Thumper (Donna Garratt) while rescuing Willard Whyte.** Right: **Jill St. John as Tiffany Case was the first American actress to play a Bond girl.**

24

to the suite via a skylight. Once inside he is greeted by a familiar voice, 'Good evening Mr Bond,' and he sees Blofeld at his desk. Then – 'Good evening Double-O Seven.' Bond is amazed to see a second Blofeld walk down the staircase towards him, 'Double jeopardy Mr Bond.' Bond remembers that he still has his bolt firing gun, but he does not know which Blofeld to kill. A white cat walks into the room and Bond sees an answer to his problem. Bond steps on the cat and it jumps into the arms of one of the Blofelds. Bond fires a bolt into the head of the Blofeld with the cat. Another white cat enters the room, but this one has a diamond necklace around its neck. 'Right idea,' says the surviving Blofeld. 'But wrong pussy,' replies Bond. Blofeld ushers Bond into an elevator down to the basement where gas escapes from a grille in the floor. Bond falls unconscious and is thrown into the boot of a waiting car by Wint and Kidd. Left for dead in an underground pipe, Bond manages to escape and leads Felix Leiter and his men to Willard Whyte, kept prisoner in his desert home by Blofeld, but not before being thrown all over the place by Bambi and Thumper. Meanwhile Tiffany has been kidnapped by Blofeld whom she spotted making his escape dressed as a woman.

Blofeld launches his satellite, and the reason why he required such a huge quantity of diamonds becomes apparent. He has had the gems fitted to a reflector dish on the orbiting spacecraft, and is now in control of a laser of unparalleled power, able to strike anywhere on earth. To demonstrate the awesome power of the laser, Blofeld causes the destruction of a Russian submarine, an American spacecraft and a Chinese missile site. By a process of elimination, Bond discovers that Blofeld is hiding on an oil rig off the coast of California.

Arriving in a parachuted balloon which 'walks' on water Bond is taken aboard the rig. Bond finds Blofeld gloating over his new mistress, Tiffany, who is stretched out on the couch. Blofeld then takes Bond on a guided tour of the control room which gives 007 the opportunity to switch the tape that directs the satellite. Unfortunately, Tiffany, not realizing Bond has already switched the tape – switches it back again. Bond is thrown in the brig, but on the way is able to release a nearby weather balloon which is the signal for Felix and Willard Whyte to attack in a fleet of helicopters. The rig is destroyed in an aerial attack while Bond uses the mini-sub containing an escaping Blofeld as a battering-ram to destroy the control room.

Safely aboard the *Queen Mary*, Bond and Tiffany indulge in a romantic evening but are interrupted by the appearance of two waiters bearing food and drink with the compliments of Willard Whyte. Although Bond has never actually seen Wint and Kidd he realizes that he is in danger when he recognizes Wint's overpowering aftershave. Wint grabs Bond from behind as Kidd advances menacingly towards him holding flaming shish kebabs. Bond breaks a bottle of brandy and throws its contents at Kidd. Engulfed in flames Kidd jumps overboard. Still struggling with Wint, Bond picks up the bomb that has fallen out of the 'bombe surprise', tucks it between the killer's legs and sends him somersaulting over the side of the ship exploding in mid-air. 'Well, he certainly left with his tail tucked between his legs.'

Looking up at the stars Tiffany turns to Bond and asks, 'James, how the hell do we get those diamonds down from there?'

Jill St. John (real name Jill Oppenheim) was the first American actress to play a leading Bond girl. Born in 1940 she made her screen debut in *Summer Love* (1958), other roles followed in *The Lost World* (1960), *The Liquidator* (1965), *Tony Rome* (1967) and *Sitting Target* (1972). She has made numerous appearances in American TV films and series including *Brenda Starr, Girl Reporter* (1974) and *Hart To Hart* (1979) with husband Robert Wagner. She had a regular cooking slot on *Good Morning America* and published *The Jill St. John Cookbook*. She is an accomplished skier and owns a boutique in Aspen, Colorado.

Lana Wood is probably best known for being the sister of the late Natalie Wood. Her appearances have been mostly limited to American TV shows including *Peyton Place*, *Long Hot Summer* and *Capitol*. She was featured in John Ford's film *The Searchers* (1956) playing her teenage sister Natalie as a little girl.

Opposite: **Bond is joined in a Vegas casino by Plenty O' Toole.** Below: **Bond convinces Marie (Denise Perrier) to tell him Blofeld's location.** Bottom: **Bond and Tiffany relax on a waterbed filled with tropical fish.**

James Bond	Roger Moore
Solitaire	Jane Seymour
Dr. Kananga	Yaphet Kotto
Sheriff Pepper	Clifton James
Tee Hee	Julius W. Harris
Baron Samedi	Geoffrey Holder
Rosie	Gloria Hendry
Felix Leiter	David Hedison
M	Bernard Lee
Miss Moneypenny	Lois Maxwell

Producers .... Harry Saltzman
.... Albert R. Broccoli
Director... Guy Hamilton
Screenplay .... Tom Mankiewicz
Director of Photography .... Ted Moore
Supervising Art Director .... Syd Cain

James Bond battles against drug king Dr. Kananga and his voodoo henchmen in his attempt to create a nation of drug dependants.

Following the murder of three British agents in 24 hours, James Bond receives an early morning visit from M and Miss Moneypenny. Quickly hiding Miss Caruso, an agent involved in his recent Italian mission, in his wardrobe, Bond is briefed by M and leaves for New York to investigate the killings. But he still finds time first to use his magnetic watch to unfasten the zip on Miss Caruso's dress.

In New York Bond is en route to meet his old friend, CIA agent Felix Leiter, when an attempt is made on his life. Meeting with Leiter, Bond learns that he is keeping Dr. Kananga, the president of the small Caribbean island of San Monique, under observation. Leiter continues his surveillance, while Bond traces his would-be assassin's car to Harlem and a restaurant called The Fillet of Soul. Once inside, Bond finds himself trapped. He has fallen into the hands of Harlem gangster Mr Big and his henchman Tee Hee. Sitting at the table dealing Tarot cards is Solitaire who, with the gift of second sight, has predicted Bond's arrival. Mr Big gives the order that the 'honky' should be wasted, and two of his men take Bond outside. After a brief struggle Bond eludes the killers and meets CIA agent Harold Strutter, who has been trailing him.

Leaving New York, Bond follows Kananga to Jamaica where he finds 'Mrs Bond' waiting for him in his hotel room. She is CIA agent Rosie Carver. With the help of Quarrel Junior, Rosie promises to show Bond where one of the agents was killed. But Bond discovers she is in the pay of Kananga and Rosie, running scared, is shot and killed by an unseen assailant. Kananga is relying on Solitaire's psychic powers to keep several steps ahead of Bond's movements, and he cannot understand her sudden change of mood. In fact, unknown to Kananga, Solitaire has forseen in the cards that she and Bond will become lovers.

During the night Bond gains entrance to Kananga's cliff-top home with the aid of a hang-glider. Once inside, he confronts Solitaire who is reading the tarot. Bond tricks her into bed using a tarot pack stacked in his favour – every card in the deck is The Lovers. The following morning, seemingly unconcerned that Solitaire has lost her powers along with her virginity, Bond dutifully goes in search of Kananga's deadly secret. He finds it – poppy fields, acre upon acre of poppy fields cover the hillside under camouflage netting, and Bond realizes that they must be destroyed before Kananga can harvest his deadly crop. However, Bond and Solitaire are spotted by an enemy helicopter which opens fire on them with machine-guns. Running for their lives, they commandeer an old double-decker bus to escape their pursuers, who are now chasing them in cars and on motorbikes. Approaching a low-level bridge at high speed, Bond slices off the top deck of the bus, which conveniently falls on the pursuing car trapping its occupants. Reaching the harbour safely, Bond and Solitaire escape with Quarrel Junior in his boat. Mr Big wants Solitaire back, and as the couple are leaving from the local airport, his men capture them. Solitaire creates a diversion, and Bond is chased in and out of the aircraft hangars by Mr Big's men, demolishing many cars and aircraft in the process but he gets away.

Bond rejoins Felix Leiter in New Orleans, where they visit the local Fillet of Soul restaurant. While Leiter is distracted with a fake telephone call, the floor opens up and Bond disappears into the basement. Bond is once more face to face with Mr Big, Tee Hee and Solitaire. Mr Big asks Bond if he has slept with Solitaire, but ever the gentleman, Bond refuses to answer to anyone except Kananga. Before Bond's eyes Mr Big's identity is torn away as Kananaga appears from under his heavy disguise. He explains that he intends to ensnare the drug population of America by giving away free samples of his heroin, thereby putting all other operators out of business and at the same time greatly increasing the number of addicts. When his poppy fields are harvested, he will increase the price of his goods – and the product

> Below left: **Bond explains the dangers of being a double agent to Rosie Carver. Below: Solitaire seeks the protection of agent 007. Right: Jane Seymour as Mr Big's seer – Solitaire.**

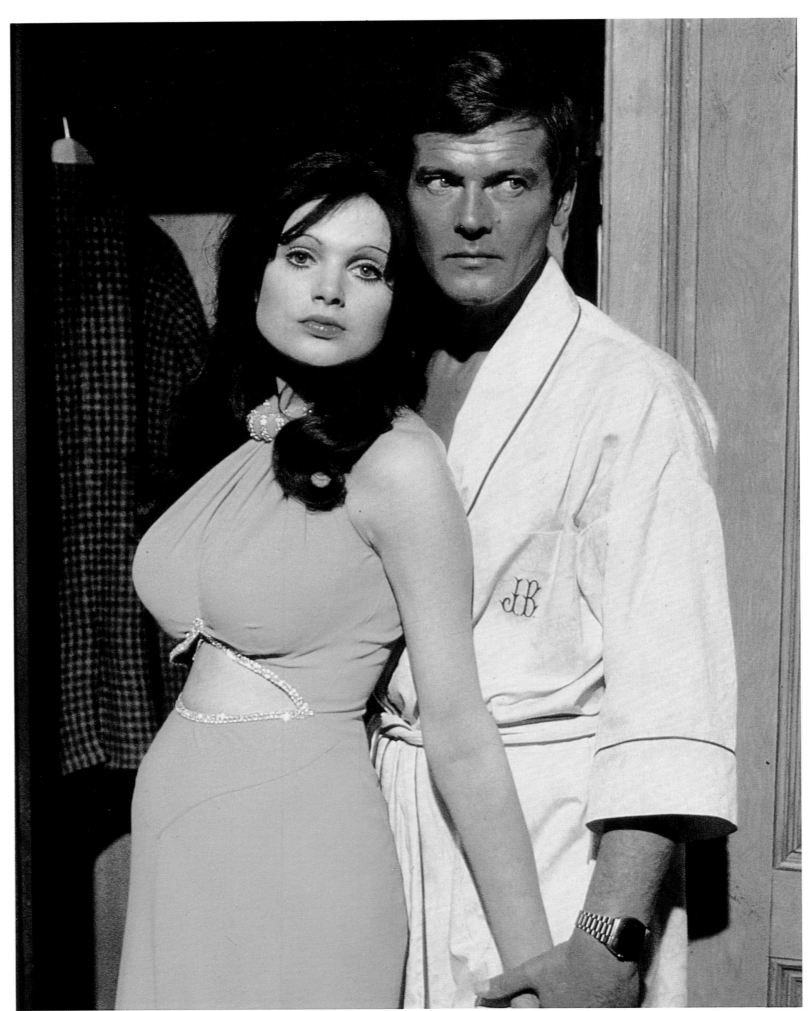

can be distributed through his chain of Fillet of Soul restaurants. His employees will be kept in check by Baron Samedi and the threat of voodoo. Bond is knocked unconscious by Tee Hee and taken to a crocodile farm, and as Solitaire is of no further use to him, Kananga decides to concoct a fitting punishment for her.

Arriving at the crocodile farm, Bond learns it is mainly a front for Kananga's drug refining activities but there are enough of the reptiles about for him to be left as lunch. Ingeniously avoiding his place on the menu, Bond makes his escape from the island stepping over the backs of the crocodiles. Setting the refining plant on fire Bond escapes in a high-powered speedboat into the nearby Louisiana bayous. But Kananga's men and the local red-neck sheriff J. W. Pepper are close on his tail. Once again Bond evades capture, but not before numerous boats and police cars are wrecked.

Under cover of night, Bond and Quarrel Junior land on San Monique. Bond rescues Solitaire from a sacrificial voodoo ceremony while Quarrel plants explosive charges to destroy the poppy fields. Finding their way into Kananga's subterranean lair, they are overcome by his guards and tied together as bait for his pet sharks. Using the motorized bezel on his wristwatch to cut himself free, Bond faces Kananga in combat. The two men fall into the shark pool where Bond forces a CO_2 gas pellet into Kananga's mouth, causing the unfortunate man to blow up like a balloon and explode.

With the mission successfully completed, Bond and Solitaire return to New York by overnight train. Unknown to the retiring couple, Tee Hee is also aboard. Breaking into their sleeping-car Tee Hee attempts to kill Bond with the pincers on his artificial arm. Bond succeeds in jamming Tee Hee's pincers on the window frame before throwing him out of the window. Reacting to Solitaire's muffled cries, Bond pulls the bunk bed out of the wall where she has been trapped during the fight. 'What are you doing, darling?' she asks. 'Oh nothing, just being disarming,' replies Bond as he throws Tee Hee's artificial arm out of the window.

The train speeds through the night with Baron Samedi sitting astride the locomotive. Perhaps the man was undead, after all?

Bond is limited to an involvement with only three women in this adventure. Cubby Broccoli had seen Jane Seymour in the BBC TV series *The Onedin Line* and thought that she was the clear choice for the role of the virginal Solitaire. Born in Hillingdon, Middlesex, Jane attended Wimbledon High School until she was 13 when she moved to the Arts Educational School to study ballet. Unfortunately, she developed cartilage trouble and was forced to abandon her chosen career. At 17 she won her first screen role in *Oh What a Lovely War* (1969) and, after leaving school, appeared in several stage productions including *The Net* and as Ophelia in *Hamlet*. She was committed to work on the *The Onedin Line*

when she was cast as Solitaire, but the BBC re-arranged her schedule so she would be free. Although Jane has appeared in films which include *Young Winston* (1972), *Somewhere In Time* (1980), and *Lassiter* (1984), she has become queen of the TV mini-series with appearances in *The Winds of War, East of Eden,* and her series *Dr.Quinn - Medicine Woman.* She has also appeared advertising a famous perfume and has published her *Guide To Romantic Living.*

Ex-Playboy Bunny, Gloria Hendry, was seen briefly as double agent Rosie Carver before becoming the obligatory sacrificial lamb in this adventure. Her other appearances include *For Love of Ivy* (1968), *The Landlord* (1970), *Across 110th Street* (1972) and *Black Caesar* (1973).

Seen escaping from a compromising situation as Miss Caruso was Madeline Smith. This child-like British actress has featured in many TV shows, usually cast as an innocent abroad and her screen career has also reflected this trend, with roles in *Taste the Blood of Dracula* (1969), *The Vampire Lovers* (1970), *Up Pompeii* (1971) and *Frankenstein and the Monster from Hell* (1973).

Opposite: **Bond relaxes with Miss Caruso (Madeline Smith).** Below left: **Gloria Hendry as the ill-fated Rosie.** Below: **Mr Big's true identity revealed – Kananga questions Bond as a frightened Solitaire looks on.**

fight with three local thugs, and discovering it missing, the girl cries, 'I've lost my charm.' 'Not from where I'm standing,' smirks Bond as he leaves her wrecked dressing-room. After examining the bullet, Q decides it could have been made only by one man – Lazar, an infamous Portuguese gun-maker living in Macao. Arriving at Lazar's shop Bond forces an answer from the shifty gun-maker when he points a nearby rifle at the man's groin and quips, 'Speak or forever hold your peace.' Not surprisingly Lazar obliges.

Bond visits the local casino where Scaramanga's mistress, Andrea Anders, is to collect another consignment of golden bullets. He follows her to Hong Kong but loses her when liaison officer, Mary Goodnight, inadvertently blocks his exit. Andrea drives off in a green Rolls Royce. Annoyed at losing his only lead, Bond discovers from Goodnight that there is only one hotel in town which uses green Rolls Royces as courtesy cars. Entering Andrea's hotel room Bond surprises her in the shower, and is surprised himself when she produces a gun. 'A water pistol,' says Bond, unruffled. After manhandling Andrea, Bond discovers that Scaramanga is due to visit the Bottoms Up Club. Bond suggests that Andrea should say nothing about their talk as Scaramanga may even use one of those little golden bullets on her, 'And that would be a pity,' says Bond, 'because they're very expensive.'

A man leaving the Bottoms Up Club is shot dead by Scaramanga. Drawing his PPK, Bond is soon arrested and taken to the partially submerged wreck of the *Queen Elizabeth* in Hong Kong harbour. Once inside, he learns that Naval Intelligence are using the old liner as their base, and arresting officer Hip is with the Service. He is surprised to meet both M and Q, and even more surprised to find the dead man was the missing scientist, Gibson. It appears that Gibson was working for Hai Fat, who probably hired Scaramanga to kill the scientist. So Bond travels to Bangkok to confront the wealthy industrialist, gambling on the chance that he has never met the killer.

Arriving at the industrialist's mountainside mansion, Bond encounters an Oriental girl, Chew Mee, swimming naked in the pool. Outraged by Bond's intrusion, Hai Fat asks him to leave but, when Bond opens his shirt to reveal a third nipple, a well known physical abnormality of the real Scaramanga, the industrialist believes him to be the hired killer. Before he leaves, Bond is invited to dinner by Hai Fat. He tells Hip of his dinner date, 'He must have found me titillating.'

Bond leaves Goodnight at the hotel and sets out for his appointment. Walking through Hai Fat's gardens, Bond is set upon by two sumo wrestlers. At first, he seems to be gaining the upper hand but is knocked unconscious from behind by the diminutive Nick Nack. Scaramanga's midget manservant is on the point of killing 007 when Hai Fat intervenes, 'Take Mr Bond to school,' he commands. 'Heaven, definitely heaven,' says Bond as he regains consciousness in the arms of several beautiful servant girls. However, Bond soon realizes that he is far from dead when he is forced into combat against two pupils of Hai Fat's martial arts academy. Bond jumps through a meshed window, and Hip's niece and her schoolgirl friends vanquish the academy's pupils. Bond makes for the river where he steals a boat,

James Bond	Roger Moore
Scaramanga	Christopher Lee
Goodnight	Britt Ekland
Andrea	Maud Adams
Nick Nack	Herve Villechaize
J. W. Pepper	Clifton James
Hip	Soon Taik Oh
M	Bernard Lee
Moneypenny	Lois Maxwell
Q	Desmond Llewelyn

Producers .... Harry Saltzman
.... Albert R. Broccoli
Director.. Guy Hamilton
Screenplay .... Richard Maibaum
.... Tom Mankiewicz
Directors of Photography.............................. Ted Moore
.... Oswald Morris
Production Designer .... Peter Murton

32

James Bond duels with Scaramanga – the man with the golden gun – to win possession of a Solex Agitator and thereby solve the problem of the world's energy shortage.

Entering M's office Bond learns that a golden bullet sent through the mail has his 007 number engraved on it. M believes the bullet has been sent by million-dollar hit man Scaramanga, and that he has been contracted to kill Bond. M suggest 007 finds Scaramanga before the hired killer finds him. Bond is also told to search for Gibson, a scientist who has disappeared with an invaluable Solex Agitator, a device which enables man to harness energy from the sun.

Bond travels to Beirut to recover the bullet that killed 002 which now graces the navel of belly dancer Saida as a lucky charm. Bond swallows the bullet during a

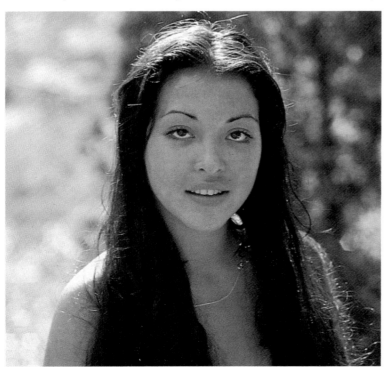

Below left: **Bond first sees Chew Mee as she swims naked in Hai Fat's pool.** Below: **Bond explains to Goodnight that Scaramanga is 'flat on his coup de grâce'.** Right: **Britt Ekland as Mary Goodnight.**

34

chased by the remainder of the academy. But, surprising them from a side turning, Bond runs through their boat, slicing it in half. When Hai Fat learns of Bond's escape, he decides to lie low but is shot dead by Scaramanga, who tells the dead man's associate, 'Mr Fat has just resigned – I'm the new chairman of the board. He always did like that mausoleum – put him in it!'

Bond meets Goodnight for dinner and is offered a complimentary bottle of Phuyuck '74. 'I approve,' says Bond. 'You do?' says a very surprised Goodnight. 'Oh, not the wine. Your frock. Tight in all the right places, not too many buttons.' Bond raises his glass for a toast. 'To this moment and the moment yet to come.' 'Oh darling I'm tempted,' says Goodnight breathlessly, 'but killing a few hours as one of your passing fancies isn't quite my scene.' Goodnight leaves as Bond is observed through binoculars by Nick Nack.

Returning to his hotel room alone and slightly dejected, Bond is pleasantly surprised to find Goodnight dressed in her nightie. 'My hard to get act didn't last very long did it?' Before Bond and Goodnight are able to consummate their desire, they are interrupted by Andrea. Bond bundles Goodnight into the wardrobe as Andrea explains she has come to warn 007 that Scaramanga knows he is in town, and it was she who sent the bullet to his headquarters. Andrea wants to leave Scaramanga, and Bond is the only man who can kill him and set her free. She tells Bond that Scaramanga talks of him with great admiration and even has a wax likeness of Bond. Determined that Bond should kill Scaramanga, Andrea offers herself to 007 and the couple retire to the bed. Andrea returns to Scaramanga's junk and Bond releases a very angry Goodnight from the wardrobe.

The next day Bond visits a Thai boxing match where he has arranged to meet Andrea. Sitting next to her Bond realizes that the girl has been shot through the chest. As Bond rifles the dead girl's handbag searching for the Solex a tall, dark man occupies the seat next to him – Scaramanga. Bond finds himself held at gun point by Nick Nack but notices the Solex hidden in the litter on the floor of the boxing hall, and manages to palm it onto the tray of peanuts carried by undercover agent Hip. Scaramanga tells Bond he has no argument with him and he will not be harmed if he stays seated until after he has left the building. Meanwhile Hip has passed the Solex to Goodnight who is investigating Scaramanga's car when she is bundled into the boot by the killer.

Unable to hail a taxi, Bond drives a new car through the showroom window only to find that he is carrying a passenger – Sheriff J. W. Pepper. The sheriff is on vacation in Bangkok and remembers Bond from the destruction he caused in the Louisiana bayous. But as he is on a mission, J. W. decides to help him. Missing a turning that Scaramanga has taken in his car, Bond does a 360 degree roll over a broken bridge to catch up with the killer. 'I've never done that before!' exclaims a breathless Sheriff Pepper as he bounces into the back seat of the car. Neither has Bond! Nevertheless, Scaramanga escapes capture when his car, fitted with wings, takes to the skies.

Scaramanga's car has been found abandoned 200 miles west of Bangkok, and Goodnight's homing signal has been tracked to a small group of islands in Red Chinese waters. M is unable to sanction 007 landing in such a delicate area, but Bond decides to pay an unofficial visit. He pilots a seaplane to the island and, on landing, is met by Nick Nack carrying a bottle of champagne. Scaramanga introduces himself by shooting the cork from the bottle of champagne. Entering the hit man's island fortress, Scaramanga shows Bond around his solar energy station which is overseen by his man Krar. Scaramanga's plan is to sell the Solex to the highest bidder and make untold millions. Showing Bond how he is also able to focus the power through a Solex gun, Scaramanga explodes Bond's seaplane. 'Now that's what I call solar power,' gloats the million-dollar hit man. 'That's what I call trouble,' retorts a worried 007. 'Mr Bond, I am now undeniably the man with the golden gun!' Bond does not argue the point.

Over lunch, Scaramanga explains that he and Bond are much the same but for the vast difference in their incomes. 'There's a useful four letter word – and you're full of it!' retorts an angry Bond. 'When I kill it is on the specific orders of my government, and those I kill are themselves killers.' Scaramanga suggests a 'duel of Titans', he and Bond should face each other man to man – his golden gun against 007's Walther PPK. As the two men stand back to back, Nick Nack starts the count. On the count of twenty, Bond turns and fires, but Scaramanga is nowhere to be seen. Nick Nack leads Bond into the hit man's funhouse explaining, 'If you kill him all this will be mine. Good shooting Monsieur Bond.' Disinclined to trust the diminutive manservant 007 admits, 'I've never killed a midget before, but there can always be a first time!'

Bond is stalked by Scaramanga through the funhouse. Bond loses his PPK as it falls to the bottom of a shaft and, drawn by the noise, Scaramanga closes in for the kill. The hit man is met with a bullet in the chest as the wax effigy that is now Bond turns and shoots him dead. Inside the complex, Bond meets Goodnight who asks where Scaramanga is, 'Flat on his coup de grâce,' quips 007. Bond discovers that Goodnight has pushed overseer Krar into the helium-cooled tanks, and his body temperature has caused the energy station to dangerously overheat. Bond enters the energy station control room to retrieve the Solex Agitator. Trying to prise the agitator from its housing, 007 is almost incinerated by the solar beam when Goodnight accidentally backs into the control panel, turning on the machine. With the agitator safely in their possession, Bond and Goodnight escape the island as the complex explodes in balls of fire.

Relaxing in the bedroom aboard Scaramanga's junk, Bond and Goodnight are interrupted when Nick Nack slips in through the ceiling. Nick Nack tries to kill Bond with a knife, but is eventually captured by 007 in a large suitcase. Screaming, 'I maybe small but I never forget,' from inside the case, Nick Nack is taken up on deck by Bond. He returns, empty handed, to the cabin and Goodnight asks, 'What did you do with him?' 'What do you think?' replies Bond. 'Oh James, you didn't?' 'Yes, I damn well did!' retorts an angry Bond. Embracing Goodnight on the bed Bond is interrupted yet again when M telephones. M asks to speak to Goodnight and Bond asks him to hold on. 'She's just coming sir!'

The junk sails towards the horizon with a forlorn Nick Nack imprisoned in the crow's nest.

Britt Ekland had wanted to appear in a Bond movie for some years and her ambition was realized when Cubby Broccoli cast her as Mary Goodnight after seeing her in *The Wicker Man* (1973). Britt was born in Stockholm, Sweden. Her career started at the age of 15 when she appeared in a toothpaste commercial. She spent two years at drama school and played small parts in films and on TV and then toured Sweden with a travelling theatre company. Britt speaks Italian, French and German as well as English and her native Swedish. She was married to Peter Sellers in 1964, and was divorced in 1968. Companion to pop singer Rod Stewart through the Seventies, she then married Stray Cats drummer, Slim Jim. They are now divorced. Her appearances include *The Night They Raided Minsky's* (1968) with Joseph Wiseman, *Get Carter* (1971) with Michael Caine, *The Monster Club* (1980) and *Scandal* (1989). She has recently appeared in the theatre in pantomime and farce.

Another native of Sweden is Maud Adams, whose 5 ft 9 ins helped begin her career in modelling. Later, she decided to branch into acting. Studying under Warren Robertson, a top American drama coach, she made her screen debut in *The Christian Licquorice Store* (1970) opposite Beau Bridges. Maud's role as Scaramanga's mistress Andrea Anders gave her great international exposure. She was to return to the Bond fold as Octopussy in 1983 (see pages 48-51).

Appearing briefly in the role of Saida the belly dancer was Carmen de Sautoy who, since appearing in the Bond movie, has developed into a serious dramatic actress. She is a member of the Royal Shakespeare Company and her recent TV credits include the Channel 4 film *Praying Mantis* and LWT's *Poirot*.

35

Far left: **Maud Adams as Scaramanga's mistress, Andrea Anders.**
Left: **Bond attempts to retrieve the remains of a golden bullet from Saida, the belly dancer.**

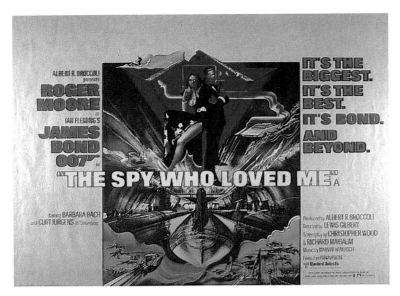

James Bond	Roger Moore
Major Anya Amasova	Barbara Bach
Stromberg	Curt Jurgens
Jaws	Richard Kiel
Naomi	Caroline Munro
General Gogol	Walter Gotell
Minister of Defence	Geoffrey Keen
M	Bernard Lee
Q	Desmond Llewelyn
Miss Moneypenny	Lois Maxwell

Producer .... Albert R. Broccoli
Director .... Lewis Gilbert
Screenplay .... Christopher Wood
.... Richard Maibaum
Production Designer .... Ken Adam
Director of Photography .... Claude Renoir

36

James Bond averts Armageddon when he battles undersea villain, Karl Stromberg.

With the disappearance of nuclear submarines *HMS Ranger* and *Potemkin*, both the British and Russian Secret Services assign their best agents to investigate. Russian KGB General Gogol contacts their top operative agent Triple X (XXX), Major Anya Amasova, and orders her to report at once. Meanwhile, inside a log cabin somewhere in the Austrian Alps, James Bond is sharing an intimate moment with a beautiful blonde, when a ticker-tape message from M tells him to pull out immediately. The girl urges Bond to stay, 'But, James, I need you.' 'So does England,' comes the loyal reply. The girl radios a KGB death squad that Bond has just left but, using his acrobatic skiing skills, he evades the Russian gunmen, killing their leader in the process.

Anya reports to General Gogol and he tells her there is a lead to follow up in Cairo. Before she leaves he tells her of the unfortunate death of her lover Sergei at the hands of the British Secret Service. Meanwhile, Commander James Bond flies to Faslane Submarine Base in Scotland for a briefing with Admiral Hargreaves. It appears that someone has developed a way of recognizing the wake of a submarine underwater and is trying to sell the microfilmed plans on the black market.

In Atlantis, the underwater marine laboratory of Karl Stromberg off the coast of Sardinia, a transaction is taking place. Stromberg is about to pay Dr. Bechmann and Professor Markovitz a vast sum of money for designing the submarine tracking system. Then Stromberg's mood changes as he explains that he has discovered someone has been trying to sell copies of the plans to opposing world powers. Asking his female assistant to leave the room before he discusses the matter, Stromberg waits for her to enter the elevator. As the door closes she falls through a trapdoor into a tank where she is devoured by a shark. So perishes anyone who would pervert Stromberg's goals for their own ends. The marine laboratory rises from the ocean bed and Stromberg calls for his two hired killers. Alone with the bulky Sandor and the seven-foot giant, Jaws, he tells them that anyone who has come into contact with the microfilm tracking system is to be eliminated. A helicopter with the two scientists takes off from the laboratory launch pad and explodes. Stromberg picks up the telephone. 'Cancel the transfer of $20 million,' comes the cold-blooded instruction.

Bond travels by camel to Cairo via a Bedouin encampment in the desert. Entering a huge tent, Bond discovers a harem of Arab beauties administering to the every whim of Hosein, a Cambridge-educated Arab and old school friend of agent 007. Hosein tells Bond that he must reach club owner Max Kalba through a contact called Aziz Fekkesh if he wants to bid for the sale of the microfilm. Accepting the hospitality of his host's harem Bond stays the night saying, 'When one is in Egypt one should delve deeply into its treasures!'

The following morning Bond visits Fekkesh's house to find he has left Felicca to keep him occupied. But Felicca is killed when she stops a bullet from Sandor's gun. Bond pushes the gunman off the roof – though not before he has told Bond where to find Fekkesh. That evening Bond arrives at the Great Pyramids of Gizah and observes Fekkesh talking with Anya. When Fekkesh sees Jaws lurking in the shadows, he panics and tries to run away – but Jaws catches up with the terrified man in a nearby tomb and kills him with his metal teeth. Bond discovers an appointment in the dead man's diary. Leaving the tomb, Bond is confronted by Anya who asks him where Fekkesh is. 'With the pharaohs,' Bond tells her as he is set upon by Ivan and Boris, her two strongarm men. Knocking both men unconscious, 007 wishes Anya goodnight hoping she has enjoyed the 'show'.

Bond meets Anya once again while visiting the Mujuba club and informs her that he knows she is agent XXX. Bond approaches Kalba to bid for the microfilm but is opposed by Anya who also wishes to place a bid. Kalba makes the keen observation, 'I see you have competition Mr Bond, and from where I sit, I fancy

Below left: **Sue Vanner keeps 007 occupied before M's message interrupts them. Below: Agent 007 is accompanied on his mission by Agent XXX. Right: Barbara Bach as Major Anya Amasova.**

you will find the lady's figure hard to match!' Kalba is called away to the telephone by a hoax and killed by Jaws. Bond leaves an 'out of order' sign on the body, and leaps through an open window into Jaws's moving van, only to be joined by Anya. She asks what happened to Kalba, Bond tells her, 'He was cut off – permanently.' Unbeknown to both Bond and Anya, Jaws is listening to their conversation from a speaker in the driver's seat. Arriving at the ancient temple ruins in the desert, Jaws attacks Bond. Then, pointing a gun at him, Anya forces Jaws to give her the microfilm which he throws on the sand. When she kneels down to pick it up, Jaws sees his chance and kicks the gun out of her hand. He takes a swing at Bond and knocks the surrounding scaffolding down on top of himself. 'Egyptian builders,' quips Bond. Anya tries to start the van and leave Bond behind – but he has the keys. They race off together as Jaws reappears and systematically pulls the van to pieces.

Travelling down the Nile on an Arab dhow Anya gasses Bond and escapes with the microfilm, but not before Bond has examined its contents. Bond discovers M, Moneypenny, Gogol and Anya using a tomb as their joint headquarters. The rival governments have decided to pool their resources in an attempt to find the missing submarines. 'We have entered a new era of Anglo-Soviet cooperation,' says Gogol, but Bond realizes that vital technical details have been deleted from the photographed plans. Bond travels to Stromberg's ocean laboratory impersonating a marine biologist. On the train journey he and Anya are once more attacked by Jaws, but Bond kicks him out of the carriage window.

Bond and Anya are met in Sardinia by Q with Bond's new Lotus Esprit. From their hotel they are collected by Stromberg's beautiful assistant Naomi and taken to Atlantis. Posing as Robert Sterling, a marine biologist, Bond is tested by the suspicious Stromberg on his knowledge of marine life. Later, Jaws confirms that Bond and Anya are the two agents he had dealt with earlier and Stromberg gives orders that they should be killed as soon as they get ashore. Sure enough, as they drive along a mountain road, Bond and Anya are attacked by a motorcyclist who fires his explosive sidecar at them. Avoiding the sidecar, Bond cuts in front of a truck carrying feather mattresses. The sidecar explodes on contact with the truck and the road is showered with millions of feathers. Unable to see where he is going, the motorcyclist rides over the edge of a cliff. 'All those feathers and he still can't fly.' Escaping a further attack from Jaws and his henchmen, Bond then takes to the water in his submersible car when machine-gunned by Naomi from her helicopter. Anya presses a button on the dashboard and a missile shoots from the car blowing Naomi out of the sky.

Left: **The impressive figure of Naomi (Caroline Munro).** Below: 007's time in Cairo is occupied by the unfortunate Felicca (Olga Bisera).

Whilst investigating Atlantis in the submersible car, Bond and Anya are attacked by frogmen in armed underwater craft. Bond successfully disposes of the enemy but has to make for dry land as his car is leaking. He drives out of the surf to the amazement of the holidaymakers on the beach, and winds down the window to eject a fish. Back at their hotel, Anya discovers Bond is responsible for the death of her lover and swears to kill 007 when their mission is over.

Bond and Anya are taken aboard the *U.S.S. Wayne*. Stromberg's super tanker, the *Liparus*, swallows the submarine and the crew is taken captive. Bond and Anya are brought before Stromberg who plans to destroy New York and Moscow with missiles from the captured submarines – global destruction will follow, he assures them. He will then build a new undersea world of which he will be ruler. Stromberg orders his guards to imprison Bond with the rest of the naval personnel and departs for Atlantis taking Anya with him. Bond kills the guards and breaks the naval crews out of the brig. Battle rages inside the hull of the *Liparus*, and Bond uses an atomic detonator to gain entry to the near impregnable control room. Once inside, he changes the co-ordinates of the missiles on the renegade submarines so that they destroy each other. With the *Liparus* exploding around them, Bond and the Russian, American and British crews crowd into the last remaining submarine. Blasting their way through the bow doors, they escape as the giant tanker sinks beneath the waves.

Bond rides to Atlantis on a wetbike to rescue Anya before the submarine has to open fire on Stromberg's headquarters. Confronting Stromberg in his state room, Bond avoids an explosive harpoon and shoots him dead. 'You've shot your last bolt Stromberg.' Cutting Anya free they leave Atlantis in a jettisoned escape pod as the first torpedo hits its mark, but not before Bond has fought Jaws one last time. Bond uses a giant magnet to catch Jaws by the teeth and drops him into the shark pool, where the seven foot giant succeeds in killing his fishy adversary and swimming away to safety. Reaching the surface in their pod, Anya points Bond's own gun at

him telling him the mission is over – but she cannot kill him. She falls into his arms instead.

Rescued by the Royal Navy, Bond and Anya are cuddling together under silk sheets to the outrage of M, Q, and Gogol. When the Minister of Defence asks, 'Bond, what do you think you're doing?' he replies, 'Keeping the British end up, sir!'

Major Anya Amasova as portrayed by American actress Barbara Bach was the first Bond girl who was the equal of Bond in every way. The two characters spend the majority of the story trying to score points against each other – and she gives Bond a good run for his money. A top model at the age of 17, Barbara's 5 ft 7 ins 35–24–35 figure was destined to grace the covers of major magazines around the world. She worked for the famed Eileen Ford Agency and it was while she was on an assignment in Rome for *Seventeen* magazine that she fell in love with Italy and a young Italian industrialist. She appeared in several Italian films before appearing in *The Spy Who Loved Me*. She is now married to ex-Beatle Ringo Starr. Her other screen appearances include *Force 10 from Navarone* (1978), *The Humanoid* (1978) and *Caveman* (1981).

Stromberg's helicopter pilot Naomi, Caroline Munro, has adorned many calendars in her years as a photographic model. She occasionally appears on TV game shows and has appeared in features including *The Abominable Dr. Phibes* (1971), *Dracula A.D. 1972* (1972), *The Golden Voyage of Sinbad* (1973) and *At the Earth's Core* (1976).

Gogol's assistant Rubelvitch was portrayed by 1969 ex-Miss World Eva Rueber-Staier. She also appeared as the same character in two other Bond films, *For Your Eyes Only* (1981) and *Octopussy* (1983). Austrian born Eva's other credits include *Carry On Dick* (1974) and *Royal Flash* (1975).

Bond has his hands full in the Austrian log cabin sequence with British girl Sue Vanner. Sue has appeared in over 300 TV commercials and her other roles include the BBC TV production of *Dracula* with Louis Jourdan.

Yugoslav actress Olga Bisera who portrayed the ill-fated Felicca retired from acting, married, and became a journalist and prolific author.

Top left: **General Gogol's assistant Rubelvitch, in the shape of ex-Miss World, Eva Rueber-Staier.** Bottom left: **Bond is in his element when he visits Sheik Hosein.** Below: **Bond and Anya search for Jaws among the ancient temple ruins.**

39

James Bond	Roger Moore
Holly Goodhead	Lois Chiles
Drax	Michael Lonsdale
Jaws	Richard Kiel
Corinne Dufour	Corinne Clery
M	Bernard Lee
Frederick Gray	Geoffrey Keen
Q	Desmond Llewelyn
Manuela	Emily Bolton
Miss Moneypenny	Lois Maxwell

Producer.. Albert R. Broccoli
Director... Lewis Gilbert
Screenplay .... Christopher Wood
Production Designer .... Ken Adam
Director of Photography .... Jean Tournier

James Bond is pitted against Hugo Drax and his diabolical scheme to repopulate the world with a race of perfect physical specimens.

An R.A.F. Boeing 747 is carrying a Moonraker space shuttle on loan from the US government when it launches from the back of the 747, destroying the aircraft. Bond is briefed on the disappearance of the Moonraker on his return from an assignment in Africa, where he narrowly escapes death at the hands of Jaws. Before Bond sets off on his mission to find the missing space shuttle, Q equips him with a deadly dart-firing wristwatch. 'Very novel, Q, you must get them in the stores in time for Christmas,' suggests 007.

Bond is collected in California by Drax's personal pilot, Corinne Dufour, on the first stage of his mission. They fly over the Moonraker complex, and in the distance Bond is amazed to see Drax's home — a magnificent French château built in the desert. He has had it shipped over and re-built brick by brick. When Bond visits

Drax in his palatial drawing-room, he is under the misapprehension that Bond has come to apologize on behalf of the British Government for the loss of his space shuttle. Paraphrasing Oscar Wilde, Drax goes on, 'To lose one aircraft may be regarded as a misfortune. To lose two seems like carelessness.' As Bond leaves, Drax tells his bodyguard Chang, 'Look after Mr Bond – see that some harm comes to him.'

Corinne takes Bond to meet Dr. Holly Goodhead. 'You're a woman,' says a surprised Bond. 'Your powers of observation do you credit Mr Bond,' says Holly. She invites Bond to try the centrifuge – a revolving arm which is used to simulate the gravity force experienced when an astronaut is shot into space. Bond asks how fast it will go. Holly explains that 3g's is equivalent to take-off pressure and most people pass out at 7. Holly is called away to the telephone by Drax as Bond's ride begins. In the control room, Chang increases the speed to 13g's but Bond disables the controls with an explosive dart from his wristwatch. Understandably reluctant to accept a helping hand from Holly, Bond stumbles dizzily from the cockpit. Recovering his balance, he notices Chang leaving the control room.

That night Bond visits Corinne's room to learn more about Drax. Corinne tells him her mother gave her a list of things not to do on a first date. 'That's not what I came for,' says 007. 'No!' says Corinne, rather surprised. Bond learns that Drax has been working on something very secret, but it has been moved. Sitting on the bed together Bond kisses Corinne. 'What about that list of your mother's?', asks Bond. 'I never learned to read,' she replies invitingly. Leaving Corinne asleep, Bond decides to investigate Drax's study. He opens the safe and is photographing some documents when he is interrupted by Corinne. Unbeknown to either of them, their intrusion has been watched by Chang.

The next morning Bond leaves Drax's estate, but not before he despatches a game warden instructed by Drax to kill him. Later, Corinne is summoned by Drax. Her employment is terminated immediately when Chang sets Drax's Doberman guard dogs on her.

Bond discovers from his photographed documents that a glass factory in Venice is manufacturing top secret components for the Drax Corporation. Arriving in St. Mark's Square, 007 determines to investigate the Venini Glass Factory and asks the receptionist if he may join the visitors' guided tour of the museum. Once inside he notices Holly is a member of the party. He follows her outside and asks her to join him for dinner that evening, but she refuses. During the day, 007 has to deal with a knife-throwing 'corpse' and water-borne gunmen, but he returns to the glass factory later that evening. In a glass-walled laboratory technicians are placing phials containing liquid into strange globes. Bond is about to investigate the contents of the phials but is disturbed by the returning technicians. Hurriedly placing a phial in his pocket he leaves another lying carelessly on a globe as he leaves the lab. As the technicians move the globe, they dislodge the phial and it falls to the floor, spilling

---

Below left: **Drax's personal pilot, Corinne Dufour. Below: After helping Bond with his enquiries Corinne falls victim to Drax's ferocious Doberman guard dogs. Right: Lois Chiles as Holly Goodhead. As a CIA agent, astrophysicist and NASA astronaut, she is well equipped to combat Jaws (Richard Kiel).**

its contents. Bond watches, horrified, as the two men die instantly. Chang attacks Bond as he returns through the glass museum. In a fight which demolishes the priceless contents of the museum, Bond eventually throws Chang to his death through a giant clock face.

Confronting Holly in her hotel bedroom, Bond discovers she is in fact, a CIA agent and, seeing an ice bucket containing champagne, he remarks, 'Bollinger. If it's '69 you were expecting me.' The two agents decide to pool their resources. M and the Minister of Defence join Bond to investigate the glass factory and the whole party dons gas masks. However, the laboratory has been moved and in its place stands a palatial office where Drax is at work. 'Excuse me, gentlemen, but not being English I sometimes find your sense of humour rather difficult to follow,' says Drax mocking the intruders. Meanwhile, with the death of Chang, Drax is in need of a new bodyguard and hires Jaws.

Landing in Rio, Bond meets his contact, Manuela. He explains to her he wants to visit Drax's warehouse that night. 'How do you kill five hours in Rio if you don't samba?' asks Bond loosening Manuela's robe. That night Bond and Manuela fight their way through carnival-packed streets to the warehouse. It appears to be empty but 007 finds a packing label marked 'Drax Air Freight'. Manuela is attacked by Jaws but he is dragged off in a party of carnival revellers. Holly arrives in Rio and she and Bond board a cable car to investigate 'Drax Air Freight' but as the cable car begins its ascent, Jaws jams the drive wheel. He climbs up the cable and onto the car. After a struggle, Bond pushes Jaws through the cable car roof, and he and Holly slide down the cable on a chain. Jaws crashes into the control station and, climbing from the wreckage, he is assisted by the diminutive Dolly. Affectionately, they walk away holding hands.

Bond has escaped the clutches of Drax's thugs, but Holly has been taken prisoner. Riding to Q's workshop on the pampas, Bond learns the phials from Drax's laboratory contained a nerve gas, highly toxic for humans but harmless to animals. The chemical formula has been derived from a rare orchid, so Bond travels by boat to where the plant was last reported seen. However, Jaws is also in the upper regions of the Tipperapi river and he leads an armed attack on 007's craft. As they approach a large waterfall Bond escapes on a hang glider, destroying his pursuers. Jaws crashes over the falls.

Back on firm ground, Bond notices a lovely girl beckoning him. He follows her through the jungle into the ruins of a Mayan temple and is greeted by yet more beautiful girls – where Drax makes his entrance. Long-term exposure to the orchid causes infertility, he explains, but he has improved on this and its seeds now yield death. Holly is also held prisoner at the temple and together they are placed in a room directly beneath the Moonraker's exhausts. They escape from threatened

incineration, steal a Moonraker and follow Drax and his other shuttles to their rendezvous in space. To their amazement, Drax has built a space station, undetectable on the radar screen. The Moonrakers dock at the space station and the two agents go aboard to disable the radar jamming system. At the same time as the first globe of nerve gas is released, both agents are captured by Jaws. Drax compares Bond's presence on the station with 'with tedious inevitability of an unloved season'.

The tension mounts as globe number two is launched and the laser is activated to destroy an American intercepting shuttle. Drax is about to have Bond and Holly expelled through the air lock, but Bond points out to Jaws that he and Dolly will not be included in Drax's rebirth of the earth. Furious, Jaws joins forces with the two agents to destroy the space station and a 'laser battle' breaks out as American spacetroopers infiltrate the headquarters. Bond shoots Drax with a poisonous dart from his watch and, inviting him to 'take a giant leap for mankind', ejects him into space. Jaws and Dolly are rescued by the American shuttle and Bond and Holly chase after the deadly globes in the last remaining Moonraker.

Bond destroys globes two and three in time but the first one launched proves more of a problem. Skirting the Earth's atmosphere the Moonraker begins to overheat and the automatic laser malfunctions. Bond switches to manual and destroys the last globe just as it is entering the Earth's atmosphere. Coming into range of an American tracking ship, the image of Bond and Holly floating in zero gravity, naked but for a sheet is beamed from the remote on board TV monitors. Watched with shock and surprise by M, Q and the Minister of Defence, the minister asks, 'My God, what's Bond doing?' 'I think he's attempting re-entry,' replies a bemused Q. Seeing the TV camera, Bond smiles and switches it off as Holly murmurs, 'Take me round the world one more time, James!'

H olly Goodhead is the most qualified of all the Bond Girls, an astrophysicist, NASA astronaut and CIA operative. She is also Bond's equal in unarmed combat, and single-handedly dispatches two of Drax's guards. Texan actress Lois Chiles won the role after sitting next to direct Lewis Gilbert on a plane. Later he remembered her and asked Cubby Broccoli what he thought and he agreed she would be excellent. Starting her career as a model she once posed for the cover of *Elle* magazine. Her other appearances include *The Great Gatsby* (1974), *Death On the Nile* (1978) and *Creepshow 2* (1988). She also appeared in TV's *Dallas* opposing the all-powerful J.R. Ewing.

Parisian Corinne Clery featured as Corinne Dufour, the unfortunate victim of Drax's killer dogs. Miss Clery first came to prominence in the controversial film *The Story of O* (1975) and also appeared in *The Humanoid* (1978) with Barbara Bach and Richard Kiel. She has a son by her first marriage.

> Left: **Bond and CIA agent Holly Goodhead board Drax's space station to disable its radar cloaking device. Below: Manuela escorts Bond through the carnival in the crowded streets of Rio. Right: Jaws finds true love in the diminutive shape of Dolly (Blanche Ravalec).**

James Bond	Roger Moore
Melina	Carole Bouquet
Columbo	Topol
Bibi	Lynn-Holly Johnson
Kristatos	Julian Glover
Lisl	Cassandra Harris
Brink	Jill Bennett
Locque	Michael Gothard
Havelock	Jack Hedley
General Gogol	Walter Gotell
Moneypenny	Lois Maxwell
Q	Desmond Llewelyn

Producer .... Albert R. Broccoli
Executive Producer .... Michael G. Wilson
Director .... John Glen
Screenplay .... Richard Maibaum
.... Michael G. Wilson
Director of Photography .... Alan Hume
Production Designer .... Peter Lamont

44

James Bond races against time to recover a Top Secret tracking system before it falls into the hands of Russian agents.

On a visit to the grave of his late wife, James Bond survives an attempt on his life by a wheelchair-bound Blofeld and dispatches the villain down a nearby chimney stack. Meanwhile, off the Albanian coast, the British spyship *The St. Georges* sinks with all hands after it strikes a floating World War II mine. Unfortunately, the sea in that area is too shallow to ensure that the secret British tracking device remains undiscovered by a foreign power. The Russians have already contacted their usual 'friend' in Greece to look into it should the device come on the market.

Returning by seaplane from a shopping spree in Athens, Melina Havelock is greeted by her parents on board their research vessel the *Triana*. Suddenly the seaplane returns and strafes the deck with machine-gun fire killing Melina's parents.

Meanwhile, at the headquarters of the British Secret Service, agent 007 is assigned to recover the missing A.T.A.C. – Automatic Targeting Attack Communicator. The machine is used as an ultra-low frequency coded transmitter to launch British submarine ballistic missiles. If the transmitter were to fall into the hands of the enemy, it would mean every order could be countermanded – or worse, British submarines could be ordered to attack their own cities. Bond must find Hector Gonzales, the pilot who murdered the Havelocks, and apply whatever pressure is necessary to discover who hired him.

Bond investigates the hit man's villa in Spain but is captured by guards. Gonzales orders him taken away to be killed when he recognizes Bond as an intelligence agent, but Gonzales himself is perforated by a crossbow bolt as he dives into his swimming pool. Bond uses the diversion to escape and catches the owner of the crossbow – the Havelock's daughter Melina. Safe in Melina's hotel room, Bond advises her to forget her quest for vengeance telling her, 'The Chinese have a saying: before setting out on revenge you first dig two graves.' Melina is unimpressed, 'I don't expect *you* to understand, but I'm half Greek – and Greek women, like Electra, always avenge their loved ones!'

Bond tracks down Emile Locque, the pay-off man at Gonzales's villa, to Cortina where the man is working for Greek smugglers. Bond's contact, Ferrara, introduces him to Anglophile Aris Kristatos who is watching his protégée, ice-skater Bibi Dahl go through her paces. He tells Bond that Locque is the right hand man of Columbo – a smuggler, white slaver and specialist in contract murder, known in the Greek underworld as 'the Dove'. On the way to his hotel Bond is just in time to save Melina from the murderous intentions of two black-suited motorcyclists. He tells her it will be safer for her to return to the *Triana*. Returning to his hotel, Bond is astounded to find Bibi waiting for him in his bed. Bond tells her to get her clothes on and he will buy her an ice-cream. He escorts Bibi to the biathlon where they watch another of her 'conquests' Eric Kreigler take part.

Bond, skiing back to his hotel, is ambushed by Kreigler and then chased by the two motorcyclists. He escapes the clutches of his pursuers and drives to the indoor ice rink with Ferrara. Before he leaves he is attacked by three hockey players. Bond wins three nil. Back at his car he finds Ferrara, murdered, and clutching a dove emblem.

Bond travels to Corfu and, dining with Kristatos at the local casino, they witness a 'scene' between Countess Lisl and Columbo. As the Countess leaves, it is apparent that she wants Bond to follow. Although it could be a trap, Bond escorts Lisl to her beach-house. The following morning Bond and Lisl are strolling along the beach when they are surprised by Locque and his man Claus in beach buggies. Lisl is run down and killed by Locque, and Claus holds 007 at gunpoint. But Claus is himself killed by a group of men wearing wet suits bearing the dove emblem.

Below left: **Cassandra Harris as the ill-fated Lisl.** Below: **Bond and Melina prepare to board the *Neptune* submarine.** Right: **Melina prepares to 'perforate' Kristatos.**

46

Bending over Lisl's body, Bond is knocked unconscious. When he regains consciousness Bond is aboard ship. He is taken to Columbo's cabin and the smuggler explains that it is Kristatos he wants, and Locque is *his* man. 'Why should I believe you?' asks 007. 'I'll prove it to you!' promises Columbo returning Bond's PPK. 'Tonight we'll go to his warehouse in Albania.' Columbo explains that Kristatos worked as a double agent during the fighting in Crete in World War II, and now works for the Russians against both their countries.

Bond and Columbo's men sail to the wharf and attack the warehouse but Locque detonates a bomb, destroying the building. His attempt to escape up a tunnelled mountain road is cut off when he is wounded by Bond. His car swerves off the road to hang precariously on the cliff edge. Bond approaches Locque holding a dove badge. 'You left this with Ferrara,' says a grim-faced 007. Tossing the badge to Locque, Bond kicks the car over the cliff edge. 'He had no head for heights!'

Bond swims to meet Melina on the ocean floor, where they leave her air tank. They decide to investigate the wreck of the *St. Georges* in the two-man submarine, *Neptune*, and discover the A.T.A.C. to be undamaged. They are attacked by a man in a diving suit whom Bond dispatches with the aid of the explosive timer from the attack communicator. However, in their absence, the *Triana* has been overrun by Kristatos and his men and Kristatos is intent on having some sport with his captives. Hoping to attract sharks, Kristatos has Bond and Melina tied together and dragged over the razor-sharp coral. The captives dive deep, and 007 lashes the rope around a large piece of coral. Kristatos's boat strains and the rope snaps. Bond and Melina hide on the sea bed breathing from her air tank until Kristatos believes them devoured by sharks.

Bond discovers the A.T.A.C. has been taken to St. Cyril's. Enlisting the assistance of Columbo and his men, 007 prepares to make a back-breaking climb to the deserted monastery which Kristatos is using as a hideout. After killing a guard who succeeds in 'getting the drop' on him, Bond winches Melina, Columbo and his men up to the monastery. Bond and Columbo surprise the guards and in the ensuing fight, Bond crashes through a window taking the guard with him, only to be confronted by the imposing figure of Eric Kreigler. 007 is saved by Bibi when she hangs on to Kreigler's gun-arm, but is slapped to the ground by the big man. Bond is on the receiving end of some hefty punches from the KGB strongarm man, when Kristatos retreating to safety with the A.T.A.C., distracts Kreigler and Bond pushes him through a window to his death. Columbo engages Kristatos in a

desperate struggle, and the A.T.A.C. falls to the ground, to be picked up by Bond. Reminding Melina about 'those two graves' Bond prevents her from killing Kristatos who, unnoticed by 007, has pulled a stiletto. Just in time, Columbo's knife thuds into his back. General Gogol arrives by helicopter to purchase the attack communicator. As Gogol approaches, Bond throws the A.T.A.C. over the cliff. 'That's detente comrade. You don't have it, I don't have it,' smiles Bond.

Returning to the *Triana*, Bond and Melina swim naked in the moonlight.

'Don't tell *me* what to do!' says Melina Havelock to James Bond, a liberated woman with a Ph.D. degree in marine archaeology. Born in 1957, French actress, Carole Bouquet, was educated at a convent school. She studied briefly at the Sorbonne University, but decided to try acting, and attended the National School of Theatre at the Paris Conservatoire. She left the Conservatoire for the starring role in Luis Bunuel's *That Obscure Object of Desire* (1977). She won rave reviews on both sides of the Atlantic and the picture was nominated for an Academy Award. Her other appearances include *Buffet Froid* (1979) [U.S. title *Cold Cuts*]. At present she is the Chanel girl, succeeding Catherine Deneuve – who once turned down the offer to appear as a Bond girl.

Born on December 13, 1958 in Glenview, Chicago, Lynn-Holly Johnson always wanted to ice-skate and had an impressive career as an amateur ice figure-skater before turning professional when she joined the Ice Capades Show in 1977 as principal performer. The precocious man eater Bibi Dahl was only her third screen role. Her other features include *Ice Castles* (1978) and *Watcher in the Woods* (1979).

Australian actress Cassandra Harris portrayed Columbo's ill-fated mistress Lisl. In her native Australia she co-hosted her own live TV chat-show called *Beauty and the Beast*. She toured with the National Theatre and appeared in commercials and TV shows such as *Enemy at the Door*. Her other screen appearances include *The Greek Tycoon* (1978) and *Rough Cut* (1980). Wife of the fifth 007, actor Pierce Brosnan, she died of cancer in January 1992, the day after their 11th wedding anniversary.

Left: **Bond and a bevy of pool beauties.** Below: **Bond and Melina fight for their lives when Kristatos has them keel-hauled over the coral reef.** Right: **Bibi Dahl continues her exercises in Kristatos's hideout on St. Cyril's.**

James Bond	Roger Moore
Octopussy	Maud Adams
Kamal Khan	Louis Jourdan
Magda	Kristina Wayborn
Gobinda	Kabir Bedi
General Orlov	Steven Berkoff
Q	Desmond Llewelyn
M	Robert Brown
Miss Moneypenny	Lois Maxwell
Gogol	Walter Gotell
Vijay	Vijay Amritraj

Producer .... Albert R. Broccoli
Executive Producer .... Michael G. Wilson
Director .... John Glen
Screenplay .... George MacDonald Fraser
.... Richard Maibaum
.... Michael G. Wilson
Director of Photography .... Alan Hume
Production Designer .... Peter Lamont

James Bond uncovers a plot to detonate an atomic bomb on an American air base by a renegade Russian General and an ex-Afghan Prince.

James Bond reports to the offices of the British Secret Service after successfully completing an assignment in South America with the sultry Bianca. Much to Moneypenny's annoyance, 007 hands a bunch of carnations to Penelope Smallbone, Moneypenny's young and beautiful new assistant. Agent 009 has been found dead in West Berlin, clutching what appeared to be a priceless Fabergé egg. On closer inspection the ornamental egg was proven to be a fake. M tells Bond he is to accompany Jim Fanning – the Service's art expert – to Sotheby's where an

identical egg is on auction. The sale of the egg could be a covert operation by the Russians attempting to raise currency for payoffs. Bond and Fanning must try to identify the seller.

Meanwhile, at a high ranking Russian disarmament meeting in the Kremlin, General Gogol is arguing against the folly of General Orlov's proposal to use armed aggression against NATO forces in Europe. Later, at the Kremlin Art Repository, Orlov learns that the fake egg has been stolen in transit – the genuine egg must be returned, whatever the cost.

At the auction, Bond and Fanning notice the arrival of a beautiful blonde who joins a dark man. Fanning tells Bond the man is 'Kamal Khan, usually a seller, marginal politician, dubious sources'. Khan opens the bidding for the egg and Bond bids against him to see how high the man will go. Khan raises his bid to half a million pounds and Bond has his answer. Bond, however, has switched the original egg for the fake. A legitimate buyer would complain at being sold a fake, but Khan – Bond thinks not!

Bond follows Khan to Delhi. Sadruddin, head of Station I, and his assistant Vijay meet 007 and Vijay later observes him engage Kamal Khan in a game of backgammon. Using the genuine egg as surety, Bond defeats Khan with his own weighted dice. Khan is not amused. 'Spend the money quickly Mr Bond,' says Khan threateningly. Bond and Vijay are soon attacked by thugs led by Khan's bodyguard Gobinda and, escaping through a camouflaged billboard, they find themselves in Q's portable workshop. Q conceals a microphone homing device inside the Fabergé egg, and equips Bond with a pen that releases acid, and a radio-directional watch which will enable him to track the egg.

That evening Bond has dinner with Magda, Khan's blonde associate. The couple retire to Bond's bedroom where, seeing a tattoo of an octopus on Magda's buttock, Bond asks, 'Forgive my curiosity, but what's that?' 'Oh that's my little Octopussy,' replies Magda. Magda steals the egg from Bond's coat pocket and slides down from the balcony using her sari to be driven away in Khan's waiting car. Bond is knocked out by Gobinda and regains consciousness to find himself a prisoner at Khan's home – the Monsoon Palace. Using the acid from his pen Bond escapes from his room, when he sees a helicopter land carrying General Orlov. Homing in on the egg, Bond learns more of Khan and Orlov's plan but the homing device is revealed when, believing the egg that Khan has recovered to be the fake, Orlov smashes it. Bond's escape is discovered and Khan, Gobinda and a group of tribesmen track Bond through the jungle. Braving a tiger, leeches and crocodiles, Bond finally escapes on a tourist boat.

Bond learns from Q that Magda's tattoo is connected with a fabulously wealthy woman. She is known as Octopussy and lives in the Floating Palace with her female entourage. 'Sexual discrimination', cries Bond, learning that men are not allowed on Octopussy's island. 'I'll definitely have to pay it a visit,' he says, raising an eyebrow. As good as his word, Bond steals into Octopussy's palace unaware she is watching him on close circuit TV. 'Am I your target for tonight?' asks Octopussy

---

Below left: **Gogol's assistant Rubelvitch (Eva Rueber-Staier).** Below: **Bond meets Octopussy at her lavish floating palace.** Right: **Maud Adams as Octopussy.**

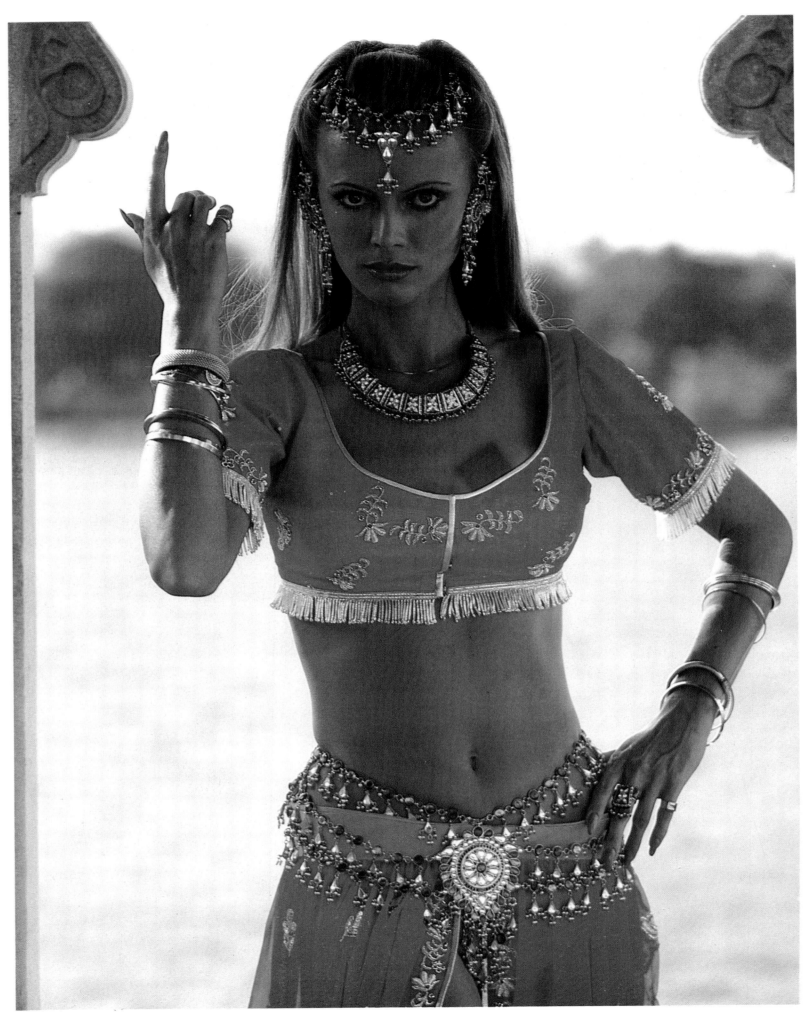

as Bond enters her quarters. Bond learns her nickname was given to her as a child by her father, not only an expert on octopuses, but a man Bond had been sent to arrest many years ago. Octopussy became involved in smuggling when her father's old contacts approached her with a commission. Since then she has diversified into shipping, hotels, carnivals and circuses. Later that night, in bed, Bond and Octopussy are attacked by thugs hired by Khan. Although 007 successfully dispatches the villains, he crashes through a window with the last surviving intruder. Allowing Octopussy to believe he has been killed by a crocodile, Bond returns to shore to hear bad news – Vijay has been murdered by the thugs whilst on watch.

Octopussy's circus next appears in Karl Marx Stadt, so Bond travels to East Germany. Octopussy and Khan entertain Orlov but Bond overhears that Khan and Orlov plan to switch the last carriage of the travelling circus train without Octopussy's knowledge. She believes the circus cannon will contain a fortune in gems. It will in fact carry an atomic bomb. Bond is attacked by one of the twins in a deadly knife throwing duo. Disposing of the twin, he is surprised by General Orlov. At gunpoint the General confesses that he intends to explode the bomb on an American air base, explaining there will be no fear of reprisals as everyone will assume it was an American bomb triggered accidentally. Europe will insist on unilateral disarmament and leave every border undefended for the Russians to walk across at will. They are disturbed when a Russian guard enters the carriage door. Bond shoots him dead but, seizing his chance, Orlov escapes. Bond steals Orlov's car and, with the tyres shredded by machine-gun bullets, Bond takes the car onto the rails and drives after the speeding train. The car is switched to the opposite side of the tracks and Bond jumps onto the train just as an oncoming train smashes his car from the tracks. Meanwhile, Orlov has driven to the border in an attempt to reach the train, but is shot by West German guards.

Bond – disguised in a gorilla suit – watches as Gobinda sets the bomb's timer. But Bond is discovered and a desperate struggle ensues on the roof of the train. The

second twin in the deadly knife throwing duo appears on the carriage roof. He and 007 fall from the speeding train and Bond kills him with one of his own knives. Disguising himself as a clown, Bond enters the big top in an attempt to defuse the bomb. Unable to convince the base commander of the danger, 007 is restrained by security guards until Octopussy shoots the lock off the cannon to reveal the bomb countdown. Bond removes the detonator only moments before the bomb is due to explode!

Khan has returned to India and Octopussy has followed him there. She confronts him but is overpowered by his guards as Magda and the island girls attack the Monsoon Palace. Bond arrives in a hot air balloon piloted by Q. Khan and Gobinda escape by horse, carrying an unconscious Octopussy to a waiting aircraft. Bond gallops after them and jumps onto the aircraft at the point of take off. Khan takes the plane into a spin in order to dislodge 007, but to no avail. He then orders Gobinda to 'Go out there and get him!' But Bond dislodges Gobinda and he falls to his death. Forcing the tail ailerons down with his feet, Bond forces Khan to bring the aircraft down on a small plateau as he and Octopussy jump from the hatch. Losing control of the aircraft, Khan plummets to his death over the edge of the plateau, crashing into the mountainside ahead.

'I wish you weren't in such a weakened condition,' says Octopussy as she and Bond relax on her barge. With that Bond relieves himself of both traction and bandages undergoing a miraculous cure. 'Oh James!' sighs Octopussy.

Maud Adams was the only actress ever to play two leading roles in a James Bond film, as well as playing the only female character to be featured as a title character in the series. A superb linguist, Maud speaks Swedish, French, German, Italian and English. She was born just below the Arctic Circle in Lulea, Sweden, on 12 February, 1945. She gave up her modelling career in 1978 and decided to concentrate all her energies into acting. Her other movie appearances include *The Hostage Tower* (1980) and *Tattoo* (1980). She also appeared with Vanessa Redgrave in the TV film *Playing For Time*, and starred regularly in the series *Chicago Story*.

Octopussy's right-hand girl Magda was another character well able to handle herself in tricky situations, and the natural athleticism of Swedish actress Kristina Wayborn was aptly suited for the role. Born on a small island in the Baltic Sea, Kristina became the Swedish track champion, and can run 100 metres in 11.3 seconds. It's a wonder that James Bond caught her at all. Kristina has had an interesting and varied career as a racing driver, a jockey and horse trainer, a wild animal trainer and clothes designer. She trained with the famous director Ingmar Bergman for three years at the Royal Academy of Stockholm, and worked under a five year contract modelling for Fabergé until being chosen by David Wolper to play Greta Garbo in the TV mini-series *Movieola*.

Left: **Kristina Wayborn as the exotic Magda.** Below: **Magda remembers Bond was the man at Sotheby's.** Bottom: **Moneypenny with her new assistant, Penelope Smallbone (Michaela Clavell).** Below right: **Bond is aided on his South American mission by the sultry Bianca (Tina Hudson).**

Has
JAMES BOND
finally met his match?

ALBERT R. BROCCOLI Presents
ROGER MOORE
as IAN FLEMING'S
JAMES BOND 007
A VIEW TO A KILL

Starring TANYA ROBERTS · GRACE JONES · PATRICK MACNEE
and CHRISTOPHER WALKEN
Music by JOHN BARRY
Production Designer PETER LAMONT Associate Producer TOM PEVSNER
Produced by ALBERT R. BROCCOLI and MICHAEL G. WILSON Directed by JOHN GLEN
Screenplay by RICHARD MAIBAUM and MICHAEL G. WILSON

James Bond	Roger Moore
Max Zorin	Christopher Walken
Stacey Sutton	Tanya Roberts
May Day	Grace Jones
Tibbett	Patrick Macnee
Scarpine	Patrick Bauchau
Chuck Lee	David Yip
Pola Ivanova	Fiona Fullerton
Jenny Flex	Alison Doody
Q	Desmond Llewelyn
M	Robert Brown
Miss Moneypenny	Lois Maxwell
General Gogol	Walter Gotell

Producers .... Albert R. Broccoli
.... Michael G. Wilson
Director.. John Glen
Screenplay .... Richard Maibaum
.... Michael G. Wilson
Production Designer .... Peter Lamont
Director of Photography .... Alan Hume

52

James Bond battles against the prodigy of Nazi experimentation and his attempt to corner the world market in microchips.

James Bond is in Siberia, recovering a microchip from the body of 003 when he has to evade Russian ski troops and escape in an 'iceberg craft' piloted by agent Kimberley Jones. 'Oh, Commander Bond,' she says as he unzips her jumpsuit. 'Call me James – it's five days to Alaska,' replies Bond suavely. Bond discovers from Q that the microchip taken from the Russian research establishment is identical to the one developed by Zorin Industries. Before this development, all

microchips had been susceptible to damage from the intense magnetic pulse of a nuclear explosion. One burst in outer space over the UK and everything with a microchip in it from the modern toaster to the most sophisticated computers – not to mention British defence systems – would be rendered absolutely useless. Realizing the Russians must have a mole in Zorin's research company Bond is ordered to make discreet enquiries.

At Royal Ascot Bond meets Sir Godfrey Tibbett, who is attached to the Service. Tibbett 'smells a rat' when Zorin's horse Pegasus wins its race, as its lineage is poor. In the winner's enclosure, Zorin, and his striking girl companion, May Day, are pointed out to Bond. Tibbett explains a friend of his, a French private detective, is investigating Zorin's background and Bond should travel to Paris to learn his progress.

Bond meets Monsieur Aubergine in the restaurant at the Eiffel Tower but the detective is killed before he can pass on all he has learned. The black-suited killer eludes 007, jumping from the tower and parachuting to a waiting speedboat. The killer was May Day, assisted by Zorin at the wheel of the speedboat.

Posing as James St. John-Smythe and with Tibbett as his chauffeur, Bond is driven to Zorin's stud farm to attend his thoroughbred sale. Bond is greeted by Pan-Ho, an oriental girl, and Scarpine, Zorin's security chief. Bond is escorted to his room in the château by Jenny Flex – leaving Tibbett to struggle with the luggage. A helicopter lands and Bond and Tibbett watch as Zorin greets its passenger – a glamorous blonde girl. That evening at a reception for the buyers Bond notices Zorin writing a cheque for his blonde visitor. Investigating Zorin's desk he discovers the cheque was for five million dollars and made payable to S. Sutton. Mingling with the guests Bond photographs Dr. Carl Mortner and oilman Bob Conley with his camera ring. Zorin introduces himself to Bond but is soon called away. When Bond begins talking to Miss Sutton, Zorin sends May Day to break up their conversation. May Day tells Zorin she is sure she has seen St. John-Smythe somewhere before.

That night Bond and Tibbett investigate Pegasus's stable and discover that his stall is an elevator, descending to a basement laboratory. Using a stethoscope, Bond cracks the safe, while Tibbett discovers that Pegasus has recently undergone surgery. An electronically operated hypodermic needle suggests that Dr. Mortner has implanted a microchip into the horse. The microchip, programmed to control an injection of additional horse steroids to overcome fatigue during a race, could be triggered by a remote control transmitter small enough to fit into the tip of a jockey's whip. Two guards notice the stall has descended into the basement and investigate. Hurriedly Bond closes the safe, but Tibbett replaces the microchip in a different compartment. Zorin's warehouse reveals a hoard of microchips, even though there is a world surplus. Bond and Tibbett dispose of the guards in packing cases on a nearby conveyor belt. Zorin is working out with May Day when they are interrupted by Scarpine with the news of intruders in the warehouse. Bond narrowly manages to regain entry to the château as Zorin raises the drawbridge, but is unable to return to his room. Zorin and May Day enter Bond's bedroom to find

Below left: **Bond shares a hot tub with Pola Ivanova.** Below: **Bond relaxes with Zorin's mysterious blonde visitor.** Right: **Tanya Roberts as Stacey Sutton.**

it empty and she remembers he was the man at the Eiffel Tower.

Returning to her bedroom May Day finds Bond in her bed. Slipping off her robe, she climbs in bed on top of him. Checking the lab, Scarpine and Dr. Mortner discover someone has opened the safe.

In the morning, Bond is called into Zorin's office. Zorin is using his desktop computer to discover Bond's true identity. Zorin smiles as Bond's image appears on his computer and the words 'James Bond 007 Licensed To Kill' flash across the screen. Zorin asks Bond to accompany him on his morning ride. In the meantime, Bond asks Tibbett to contact M and put a trace on the cheque issued to Miss Sutton. Tibbett drives into town but, taking the Rolls through the car wash, he is killed by May Day.

Zorin's morning ride turns out to be a very rough experience. 007 finds himself covering a steeplechase course where the jumps are electronically raised and lengthened, and the exercise boys try to knock him from his horse. Zorin uses the remote control transmitter on his whip to send Bond's horse wildly out of control. Chased through the woods by Scarpine and his men, Bond sees the Rolls. He jumps from his horse and hangs on to the car, only to find May Day is driving and Tibbett's body is slumped in the back seat. Bond is knocked unconscious and placed in the car with Tibbett, and May Day pushes the car into a nearby lake. The cold water rising around his body brings Bond back to consciousness and he escapes from the car. But Zorin and May Day are still standing at the lakeside, and Bond carefully breathes from the compressed air in the car tyres.

Zorin and May Day arrive in San Francisco by airship. Bond's contact there, CIA agent Chuck Lee, has identified the photographs taken by 007 at the château and reveals that Mortner's real identity is Hans Glaub, a German pioneer in the development of steroids. During World War II he experimented with steroids on pregnant women in concentration camps to enhance intelligence. Virtually every mother aborted, although a handful of children were produced with phenomenal I.Q.s. However, there was one side-effect – they were psychotic. Glaub was unable to be tried by the War Crimes Commission as the Russians grabbed him at the end of the War and set him up in a laboratory to develop steroids for their athletes. There is every chance that Zorin is the result of one of Glaub's experiments – and he is certainly psychotic.

That night Bond investigates Zorin's oil pumping station but, as 007 swims into the pipe, Zorin begins testing its efficiency, and Bond is almost drawn into the rotating blades of the pump. Bond has noticed another diver, and swimming ashore discovers it to be Pola Ivanova. They drive to the Nippon Relaxation Spa where they share a hot tub. 'That feels wonderful,' says Pola. 'Feels even better from where I'm sitting. Would you like it harder?' askes Bond massaging her neck. Pola leaves with the tape she has recorded of Zorin's conversation in the control room while Bond is showering. But Bond has switched tapes and learns that something is going to happen in Silicon Valley in three days, but is puzzled by the name Mainstrike.

Posing as James Stock from the London *Financial Times*, Bond visits San Francisco City Hall to interview W. G. Howe, who is the head of the Department of Conservation for oil and mines. Bond discovers it is usual practice to pump sea water in to test the integrity of an oil pipeline. Stacey Sutton is also at City Hall and Bond follows her to a mansion on the outskirts of town, where he convinces her he is not a 'Zorin stooge' after driving off several of Zorin's thugs who break into her house. Stacey is a geologist who works for City Hall and is heir to Sutton Oil which Zorin has taken from her in a rigged proxy fight. Knowing that her late father's oil company is worth far less than five million dollars, Stacey realizes Zorin has tried to buy her silence. 'I'd sell everything and live in a tent before I give up,' says Stacey tearing up Zorin's cheque. Stacey retires for the night, and Bond sleeps on guard in a chair. The next morning they experience a slight earth tremor and Bond mentions Zorin's water pumping activities. Stacey explains that pumping sea water into a fault area is extremely dangerous, as flooding a fault could cause a major earthquake. She then tries to explain Zorin's plan to Howe – but he fires her.

Chuck Lee tells Bond that he must know Zorin's specific intentions before he can take it to his superiors but he is murdered by May Day as he leaves Stacey's house. That evening Bond and Stacey investigate the file room at City Hall. They discover that Mainstrike is an abandoned silver mine by the San Andreas fault. Suddenly Zorin bursts in with May Day, who disarms Bond. Howe is working late in his office. Zorin shoots him with Bond's gun and traps 007 and Stacey in an elevator. Zorin and May Day set the building on fire and abandon Bond and Stacey to their fate. Climbing through the service hatch of the elevator, Bond lifts Stacey to safety, but as they leave the burning building, Bond is arrested by a police captain who has found his gun at the scene of Howe's murder. Bond and Stacey escape in a fire truck and successfully elude the policemen when they drive over a raising drawbridge.

They drive to the Mainstrike mine where the full extent of Zorin's plan is revealed. By flooding the faults Zorin can create a double earthquake, moving both fault lines at once, and submerging the whole of Silicon Valley forever. With less than an hour before the culmination of Zorin's plan, Bond has to act fast, but May Day, Jenny Flex and Pan-Ho are after him. Zorin detonates the bombs set to flood the mine, sweeping Jenny Flex and Pan-Ho to their deaths. Zorin and Scarpine machine-gun the surviving miners. Stacey escapes up a shaft to the surface, but Bond is caught by May Day as they plunge into the raging flood waters. As the water subsides, Bond and May Day make for the cavern where Zorin has planted a time bomb. If the bomb detonates, the huge amount of explosives beneath will rupture the geological lock which holds the faults together. Bond and May Day lift the bomb onto a railcar but, as they are trying to push it out of the mine, the handbrake jams. With Bond shouting at her to jump, May Day rides the railcar clear of the mine and the bomb explodes, killing her instantly.

In her excitement at seeing Bond alive, Stacey fails to notice Zorin is closing in on her in his airship. As he yanks her inside the dirigible, Bond clings to its mooring line for dear life. Zorin heads for the Golden Gate Bridge where he intends to smash Bond against its girders. Bond lashes the mooring rope around the cables on

the bridge while Stacey attacks Zorin. The airship gondola crashes into the bridge knocking Mortner and Scarpine unconscious. Stacey leaps from the gondola onto the bridge as Zorin chases her with a fire axe. Bond and Zorin struggle violently on the bridge until Zorin loses his grip and falls to his death into the water far below. Having regained consciousness and witnessing the death of his prodigy, Mortner attempts to destroy Bond with a bundle of dynamite but Bond severs the mooring rope with the axe and the airship shudders violently as Mortner falls back into the gondola. An enormous explosion destroys the airship taking Mortner and Scarpine with it.

Sharing a shower together, Bond and Stacey are interrupted by Q's robot snooper. Reporting to M, Q reports, '007 is alive – he's just cleaning up a few details!' Bond throws a towel over the snooper as he and Stacey disappear below the shower curtain. 'Oh, James,' sighs Stacey.

Tanya Robert's character, Stacey Sutton, is undoubtedly the most helpless of all the Bond Girls to date, as she hangs from Bond's arm squealing at every opportunity. While appearing in TV's *Vegas*, Tanya was seen by producer Aaron Spelling and was cast in *Charlie's Angels*. Her success in the show was immediate and she became a popular TV personality. She was the original choice to star opposite Dudley Moore in '*10*' but she was replaced at the last moment by Bo Derek. Her other movie appearances include *The Beastmaster* (1982) and *Sheena, Queen of the Jungle* (1984).

May Day was Grace Jones's second screen appearance after her debut in *Conan The Destroyer* (1984). This flamboyant and visually exciting singer/actress left her native Jamaica at the age of 18 for New York, where she worked as a model while auditioning for films and plays. She then moved to Paris and within three months was one of France's top models. Her first single, 'La Vie En Rose' went gold in France and Italy. She continued to cultivate her *avant-garde* image under the spell of French artist Jean Paul Goude. She made headline news when she hit chat-show host Russell Harty on his live TV show. Her other movie appearances include *Vamp* (1987).

Fiona Fullerton makes a brief but telling appearance as Pola Ivanova. She has one of the best lines in the film when she squeals, 'Oh, the bubbles tickle my – Tchaikovsky!' as Bond switches the cassette player on. Born in Nigeria, Fiona entered the film industry in 1968 at the age of 12 when she appeared in *Run Wild, Run Free*. Her other screen appearances include *Nicholas and Alexandra* (1971) and *Alice's Adventures in Wonderland* (1972). She has also appeared in the TV series *The Charmer, Angels* and *Dick Barton*. A recent stage success was *The Royal Baccarat Scandal*.

Opposite: **Grace Jones brings her unique style to the role of May Day.** Below: **Alison Doody as Jenny Flex.**

James Bond	Timothy Dalton
Kara Milovy	Maryam d'Abo
General Georgi Koskov	Jeroen Krabbe
Brad Whitaker	Joe Don Baker
General Leonid Pushkin	John Rhys-Davies
Kamran Shah	Art Malik
Necros	Andreas Wisniewski
Saunders	Thomas Wheatley
Q	Desmond Llewelyn
M	Robert Brown
Miss Moneypenny	Caroline Bliss

Producers .... Albert R. Broccoli
.... Michael G. Wilson
Director.. John Glen
Screenplay .... Richard Maibaum
.... Michael G. Wilson
Production Designed by .... Peter Lamont
Director of Photography .... Alec Mills

James Bond unravels a complicated plot involving a KGB General, an international terrorist and an unscrupulous arms dealer.

After disposing of an assassin who has infiltrated a training mission on Gibraltar, James Bond travels to Bratislava where he is assigned to protect the defecting General Koskov. That evening Bond attends a concert and is impressed by the attractive blonde cellist in the orchestra. His contact Saunders tells him everything is set for Koskov to make his run. Leaving the concert hall Bond and Saunders enter a closed building across the street and, once upstairs, Bond positions himself on the balcony with his sniper's rifle. He waits for the KGB sniper who will most certainly cut Koskov's run short if he does not get in the first shot. Through the telescopic sight of his rifle, Bond is surprised to see the enemy sniper is the blonde cellist. Realizing she is an amateur, Bond deliberately disobeys his orders to kill the sniper and shoots the gun from her hand. Koskov is literally shot across the border in a natural gas pipeline and flown by Harrier jet to England. 007 asks Q and Moneypenny to see if they can discover any information about the female sniper.

During his de-briefing with M at the Koskov safe house, Bond explains the note left on the body of the double-O agent murdered on Gibraltar means 'Death to Spies'. Koskov reveals that this is an assassination programme instigated by General Pushkin to remove all western agents. Unbeknown to the gathering, Necros, an international terrorist has infiltrated the house disguised as a milkman. As Bond and M leave for London, Necros strangles one guard and disposes of any further opposition with his explosive milk bottles, finally grabbing a reluctant Koskov and kidnapping him in a helicopter. After such a humiliation by the KGB, Bond is ordered to assassinate General Pushkin, but Bond knows Pushkin to be a man of integrity and doubts he would instigate such an operation. Without M's knowledge Bond returns to Bratislava to investigate the blonde cellist. Waiting in her apartment, Bond discovers that her name is Kara and that she is Koskov's girlfriend. Kara believes Bond to be Koskov's friend and escapes with him in his gadget laden Aston Martin.

In Tangier, arms dealer, Brad Whitaker, is visited at his villa by General Pushkin. Pushkin informs Whitaker that he knows Koskov and the arms dealer are planning something. He cancels his recent arms order and tells Whitaker to return the money in two days or he will put him out of business – permanently. Whitaker tells Koskov (who was kidnapped by Necros only to deceive the British) that his plan that Bond should kill Pushkin does not seem to be working. Koskov suggests the death of another British agent will guarantee Pushkin's demise.

Bond and Kara are sight-seeing in Vienna and they visit the funfair where 007 has arranged to meet Saunders. Leaving Kara on the pretext of receiving a message from Koskov, Bond keeps his appointment with Saunders in a nearby café – but Necros has booby-trapped the mechanism operating the café's sliding glass door. As Saunders leaves, Necros triggers an explosive device sending the glass door scything into the unfortunate agent. Surveying the carnage, Bond sees a balloon bearing the words 'Smiert Spionam' – 'Death to Spies'. Bond returns to Kara, who asks if he has heard from Koskov. 'Yes, I got the message,' says Bond, trying to control his anger. He tells Kara they must leave for Tangier immediately where Koskov is waiting for her. Back in Tangier, Bond questions Pushkin at gunpoint about Koskov's allegations. Satisfied that Pushkin is an innocent party, Bond is now sure of his true quarry. Bond accepts Pushkin's suggestion that Bond should fake his assassination. Believing the Soviet General is dead, Koskov tricks Kara into drugging Bond, and Koskov and Necros board a Russian transport plane, taking Kara and the drugged Bond with them. Bond and Kara are transferred to the jail of a Russian air base in Afghanistan but Bond disables the guards with Kara's help and they escape over the perimeter fence with a fellow prisoner.

Bond and Kara are captured by a local group of Mujahedin tribesmen and discover their fellow prisoner is Kamran Shah, the group's leader. Unable to enlist

---

Below left: **Dulice Liecier as CIA agent Ava. Below: Bond warms to Kara. Right: Maryam d'Abo as Kara Milovy.**

58

Kamran's help, Bond is forced to accompany the tribesman on a drug deal in the desert. At the rendezvous he discovers the buyer is Koskov, who is financing the deal with the down payment of the arms money. Hiding in the drug-laden trucks, Bond is driven back to the air base and assists in loading the cargo into the transport plane – where he plants a bomb. However, Koskov and Necros recognize him and Bond is trapped inside the aircraft. Kamran and his men attack the air base as Bond hijacks the transport plane. During the ensuing battle, Kara drives into the hold of the aircraft pursued by Necros and Koskov, and joins Bond in the cockpit as the plane takes off – unaware that Necros is aboard. Kara takes the controls while Bond returns to the hold to defuse his bomb but he is suddenly attacked from behind by Necros. Panicking at the controls, Kara accidently opens the loading ramp, and the netted cargo of drugs trails from the plane with the two men hanging on. After a desperate struggle Necros is left clinging on to Bond's boot. Drawing a knife Bond cuts his boot laces and the unfortunate killer plunges to his death. Bond then defuses the bomb, resets the timer and drops it on the Russian troops pursuing Kamran and his men. Returning to the flight deck Bond discovers the aircraft is running out of fuel. He sends Kara into the jeep secured in the hold, lowers the ramp and fires the release mechanism. As the aircraft is about to crash, the jeep is jettisoned from the rear of the plane and Bond and Kara safely crash land.

Whitaker is in his villa in Tangier where Bond finds him playing with his model soldiers. Bond is knocked to the floor and Whitacker attacks him with an armoured machine-gun. Placing his explosive keyfinder on a bust of Wellington, Bond dodges Whitaker's bullets as Q's handy gadget detonates. The bust crashes down on the arms dealer killing him instantly. 'He met his Waterloo,' Bond says dryly to Pushkin as he enters the room. Koskov is apparently overjoyed at seeing Pushkin but his good humour is short lived when the Soviet General orders him sent home – in the diplomatic bag!

After a hugely successful concert, Kara returns to her dressing-room and is overjoyed to find that Bond has not missed her performance after all.

Kara Milovy is unusual for a Bond Girl in that she is a more vulnerable and naïve character than the kind of woman that 007 usually associates with, and this is probably the reason why James Bond warms to her character. Born in London of a Dutch father and a Russian (Georgian) mother, Maryam d'Abo left England at the age of five and was brought up and educated in Paris and Geneva. French is her mother tongue, although she speaks English fluently without a trace of an accent. She claims it was her reaction to the Bond movies at the age of eleven that made her want be an actress. Maryam returned to London in 1980 to study at the Drama Centre, and has since appeared in such films as *White Nights*, *Lime Street* and *Until September*. She has also appeared on TV in commercials and the mini-series *Master of the Game*.

After twenty-five years and fourteen films *The Living Daylights* introduced us to a new Miss Moneypenny in the shape of National Theatre player Caroline Bliss. Caroline originally studied dancing but later trained at the Bristol Old Vic School. Her first television role was Princess Diana in *Charles and Diana, a Royal Love Story* for ABC TV in America. Her other TV appearances include *Chess Game*, *My Brother Jonathan* and *Dempsey and Makepeace*. She is the grand-daughter of composer Sir Arthur Bliss, Master of the Queen's Music.

Opposite top: **After dealing with Pushkin, Bond uses Rubavitch (Virginia Hey) to distract the General's guard as he enters the room.** Opposite below: **Linda (Kell Tyler) is bored – until the arrival of 007 by parachute.** Below: **Catherine Rabett as CIA agent Liz.** Below left: **James Bond and Miss Moneypenny watch as Q demonstrates his latest gadget, a portable rocket-firing radio which he gleefully describes as a 'ghetto blaster'.** Bottom: **Once again, 007 is surrounded by a bevy of beauties.**

59

His bad side is a dangerous place to be.

TIMOTHY DALTON
JAMES BOND 007
LICENCE TO KILL
COMING JULY '89
UA

James Bond	**Timothy Dalton**
Pam Bouvier	**Carey Lowell**
Franz Sanchez	**Robert Davi**
Lupe Lamora	**Talisa Soto**
Milton Krest	**Anthony Zerbe**
Joe Butcher	**Wayne Newton**
Q	**Desmond Llewelyn**
Felix Leiter	**David Hedison**
Della Churchill	**Priscilla Barnes**
M	**Robert Brown**
Miss Moneypenny	**Caroline Bliss**
Heller	**Don Stroud**

Producers .... Albert R. Broccoli
.... Michael G. Wilson
Director .... John Glen
Screenplay .... Michael G. Wilson
.... Richard Maibaum
Production Designed by .... Peter Lamont
Director of Photography .... Alec Mills

60

James Bond sets out on a personal vendetta against a billionaire drug lord in South America.

James Bond is on leave in the Florida Keys where he is about to be the best man at the wedding of his old CIA friend, Felix Leiter, to Della Churchill. On their way to the church in Key West, Bond, Leiter and his fisherman buddy, Sharkey, are stopped by a Coast Guard helicopter swooping down to report that billionaire drug lord Franz Sanchez is at this moment within reach in the nearby Bahamas. Leiter, who has left the CIA and is now in charge of the Drug Enforcement Agency office in the south of Florida, has been desperate to get his

hands on Sanchez – a vicious criminal, invulnerable under the protection of bought politicians in a small banana republic in Latin America. Now armed with extradition papers, Leiter has a real chance to capture his nemesis. The wedding must wait. Leiter, with Bond's help, captures Sanchez after an exciting land and air chase that ends with Bond literally reeling in Sanchez's single-engined aircraft while dangling beneath the Coast Guard helicopter. Bond and Leiter eventually arrive at the church by parachute!

No sooner is Sanchez in custody than a cleverly organized escape is engineered. The leader among them is Milton Krest, who operates out of Key West behind the cover of a marine biology laboratory and the research vessel the *Wavekrest*. Sanchez returns to safety in his Latin American headquarters in Isthmus City, but not before exacting a horrible revenge on Leiter and Della. As Bond is about to fly back to London to return to duty, he learns of Sanchez's escape and immediately drives to Leiter's home where he discovers Della dead and Felix mutilated and barely alive. Certain that not enough will be done by the Drug Enforcement Agency, because of the extradition problem, Bond decides to go after Sanchez on his own – he will make it his personal mission to bring down the vicious drug lord and is willing to sacrifice his own career as double-O agent, if necessary.

When M arrives in Key West to remind Bond that the capture of Sanchez is an American matter and to forget about it, Bond refuses and is told that his licence to kill is summarily revoked and to hand in his PPK. Bond refuses, eludes his fellow agents, and sets off on his own. Learning from Sharkey that Leiter's wounds were most probably caused by a man-eating shark Bond, with the help of the burly fisherman, follows a trail that eventually leads to Krest's marine biology lab. He not only discovers it is where Leiter was tortured but finds the renegade U.S. Marshall Killifer who, thanks to a two million dollar bribe, was a key player in arranging Sanchez's clever escape. Bond makes certain that Killifer is killed by the same shark that attacked Leiter.

Bond's next move is to slip aboard the *Wavekrest* in the hope that it will lead him further into the heart of the Sanchez drug empire. He encounters the seductive and beautiful Lupe, Sanchez's sometime girlfriend. Though always in fear of Sanchez and his fits of murderous temper, she agrees to help the handsome stranger.

In Isthmus City Sanchez owns not only the casino, but the banks and practically everything else, including the corrupt government run by President Hector Lopez. Bond enlists the aid of one of Leiter's key contacts, the exquisite Pam Bouvier, a freelance charter pilot who has flown for both the U.S. Army and the CIA front, Air America. Bearing suitcases stuffed with millions of dollars of drug money 'recovered' from the *Wavekrest*, Bond and Pam fly to Isthmus City where they set up residence in style in a luxurious suite in the top hotel. He quickly discovers that Sanchez's bank and gambling casino are fronts for a sophisticated money-laundering operation. Among Sanchez's principal accomplices are his financial adviser Truman-Lodge, knife-throwing thug Dario and a former American Green Beret, Colonel Heller. As a means of broadcasting drug-dealing prices to his

---

Below left: **Bond gets to know Lupe Lamora.** Below: **007 gets the drop on Pam Bouvier.** Right: **The latest in the long line of Bond girls – Carey Lowell as Pam Bouvier.**

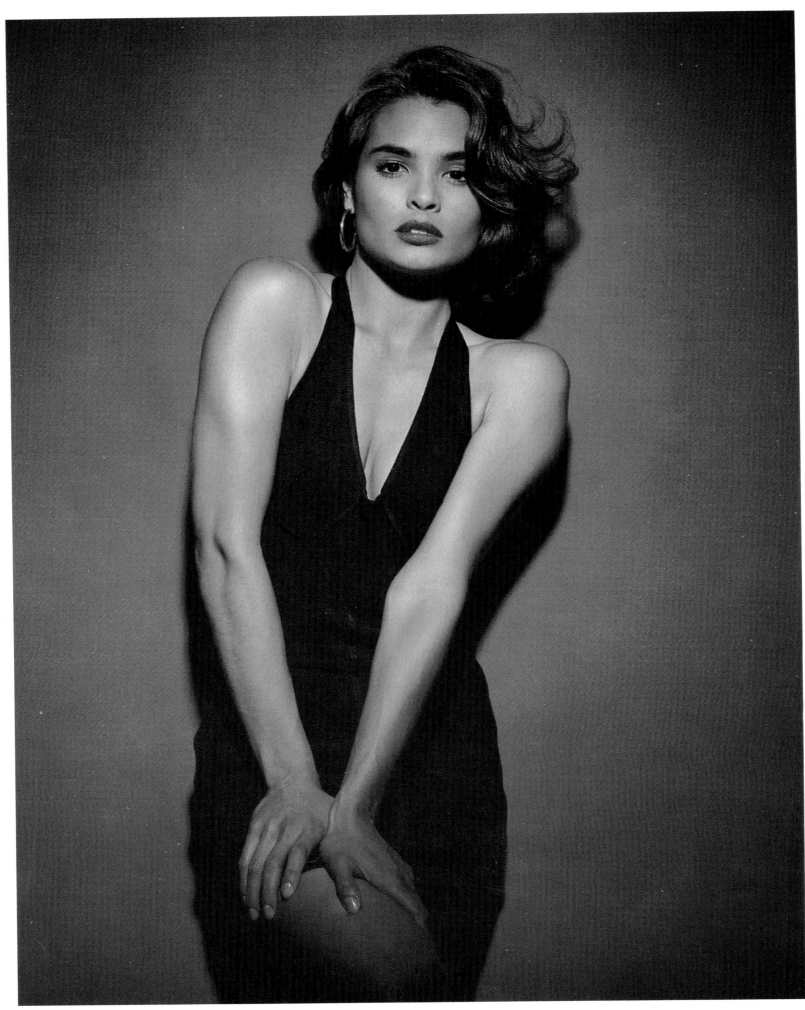

international network, Sanchez works through a flamboyant television fund-raiser named Joe Butcher, leader of a cult espousing the secrets of 'cone-power', headquartered at the nearby Olimpatec Meditation Institute. As part of his plan to enlarge his evil empire to every corner of the globe, Sanchez arranges for a group of Oriental businessmen headed by Kwan to arrive for discussions about collaborating with his organization in order to bring the drug trade in all Asia under his control.

At the gambling casino with his 'secretary' Pam, Bond uses the pliable Lupe to arrange a meeting with Sanchez. 007 readily discloses his true identity and his present situation, a former British agent seeking employment with a generous patron. Sanchez is intrigued but advises Bond that he has all the help he needs. While Bond plots how to break through Sanchez's formidable defences, reinforcements arrive from London. Moneypenny has told Q of the reasons for Bond's dismissal from the Service, so Q decides, without authorization, to take his holiday leave and shows up in Isthmus City with a bag of lethal tricks. Bond sets upon a plan to kill Sanchez and is about to pull the trigger when he is unexpectedly captured by Kwan and his accomplice Loti. They are undercover narcotics agents from Hong Kong and have spent years to reach the point where they have finally been able to penetrate the Sanchez organization. Bond's 'rogue-agent' theatrics have threatened to blow their plan of penetrating the heart of Sanchez's drug kingdom. Bond killing him would not stop his trade in death! Suddenly Heller with a detachment of the Isthmus City army arrive at the safe-house and Kwan and his people are annihilated.

Heller and Sanchez find 007 among the rubble and Sanchez, now convinced of Bond's sincerity, takes him to his palatial home to recover. Knowing that the *Wavekrest* is about to dock in Isthmus City, Bond is able to persuade Sanchez that Milton Krest has been double-crossing him. Bond cleverly does a 'sting' on Krest, and as a result Sanchez sends him to a horrible death. Reluctantly, Bond accepts Q's desire to be a field operative for the first time, and together with Pam and Lupe, each in their own way helping him, they slowly begin to chip away at the very foundations of Sanchez's organization. Sanchez decides to clinch his deal with the Orientals by showing them the heart of Joe Butcher's Olimpatec Meditation Institute. Still considering Bond as a loyal lieutenant, he brings him along to assist in a major operation he has planned. Beneath the institute is a secret laboratory where Sanchez has ingeniously had research chemists successfully working on a formula that would allow cocaine to be dissolved in gasoline which could then be converted back to powder. Until it reached its destination, it appears to be no more than an innocent shipment of petrol. A fleet of tanker trucks are being prepared to transport the shipment to the coast to be loaded on ships heading for the Orient.

Bond finally shows his hand and Sanchez realizes that his 'friend' is really his deadly enemy as the convoy heads for port with its lethal cargo. With the help of

Pam, flying a tiny crop-duster aeroplane, Bond eventually faces Sanchez in a bloody duel to the death, but not before Bond makes certain that Sanchez knows that it has all been personal.

Born on 11 February 1961 in New York, Carey Lowell was one of America's leading fashion models working with top designers Calvin Klein and Ralph Lauren. She began modelling part time while attending the University of Colorado, and it was during this time that her 5 ft 10 ins caught the attention of a representative of the prestigious Ford Model Agency in New York. She lived in France for a brief period before deciding to continue her college education and modelling career. She won the part of Pam Bouvier after an extensive search for the first Bond Girl embodying the spirit of the 1990s. Her acting début was in *Club Paradise* (1986) with Robin Williams and soon after she appeared in *Dangerously Close* (1986), *Downtwisted* (1987) and *Me and Him* (1988).

Licence To Kill is only the second screen appearance for leading American fashion model Talisa Soto. Her first was in *Spike of Bensonhurst*, directed by cult director Paul Morrissey. At the age of fifteen with no previous experience, Talisa became a fashion model with one of New York's top agencies. She literally walked in off the street, looking for a summer job. Within a week, she was in Paris being photographed by Bruce Weber for *Vogue* magazine. Born Miriam Soto in Brooklyn on 27 March 1967, she has decided to cut down on her modelling work while concentrating on her film career. It is her ambition to be 'an incredible actress'.

Opposite: **Talisa Soto** as the pliable Lupe Lamora. Below left: **Caroline Bliss** in her her final appearance as Miss Moneypenny. Below: **Diana Lee-Hsu** as Loti, the beautiful and deadly Hong Kong undercover narcotics agent.

You know the name   You know the number

GOLDENEYE

James Bond	Pierce Brosnan
Alexander Trevelyan	Sean Bean
Natalya Simonova	Izabella Scorupco
Xenia Onatopp	Famke Janssen
Jack Wade	Joe Don Baker
Valentin Zukovsky	Robbie Coltrane
Mishkin	Tcheky Karyo
Ourumov	Gottfried John
Boris Grishenko	Alan Cumming
Tanner	Michael Kitchen
Caroline	Serena Gordon
Q	Desmond Llewelyn
Miss Moneypenny	Samantha Bond
Irina	Minnie Driver
and	
M	Judi Dench

Producers .... Michael G. Wilson
.... Barbara Broccoli
Director .... Martin Campbell
Story .... Michael France
Screenplay .... Jeffrey Caine and Bruce Feirstein
Production Designed by .... Peter Lamont
Director of Photography .... Phil Meheux

64

James Bond battles with renegade Russian forces who threaten to destroy the world's social and financial fabric with the aid of an outer space weapons system, code-named GoldenEye.

Bond and 006, his friend and colleague Alec Trevelyan, join forces to penetrate a secret, mountain-top Soviet Nerve Gas Facility. They are detected and Trevelyan is captured by Commander Ourumov. Bond escapes, grabbing a military motorcycle and taking off in a hail of Russian bullets to pursue a light plane heading towards take-off from the landing strip hundreds of feet above the valley floor. As the limpet mines Bond planted earlier explode, destroying the chemical factory, the aircraft surges over the edge of the precipice and James Bond accelerates after it, over the cliff edge.

Nine years later, Bond is behind the wheel of his Aston Martin DB5, speeding along the mountain roads above Monte Carlo. His attractive passenger is Caroline, sent from London by the new M to complete an evaluation on 007. In his rear view mirror, Bond notices a red Ferrari racing towards him, driven by a ravishingly beautiful woman. Driving parallel, Bond and the mystery woman exchange smiles and begin a duel of driving skills. Finally, Bond is outmanoeuvred by his unknown opponent and she accelerates away into the distance.

That evening, Bond arrives at the casino in Monte Carlo to find the red Ferrari parked outside and its mystery driver within. Bond buys her a drink, introduces himself at the baccarat table and discovers with some amusement that she is Georgian-Russian and called Xenia Onatopp. Everyone has declined to bet against Xenia until Bond calls 'Banco'. 'It appears we share the same passions. Three, anyway,' suggests Bond. 'I count two,' replies Xenia, 'motoring and baccarat. I hope your third is where your real talent lies.' Before they can continue their conversation, Xenia leaves with Canadian Admiral Chuck Farrell.

Below left: Serena Gordon as Caroline, sent by M to complete an evaluation on 007. Below: James Bond (Pierce Brosnan) keeps an eye on the decidedly deadly Xenia (Famke Janssen). Right: Computer programmers don't come prettier than this – Izabella Scorupco as Natalya.

Bond receives a message from Moneypenny via the onboard computer system in his DB5, and discovers Xenia is an ex-Soviet fighter-pilot with suspected links to the Janus Crime Syndicate located in St Petersburg. Later that night, on the luxury yacht *Manticore*, Xenia kills Farrell in her own special way – as they make love, she crushes his spine between her thighs. With an accomplice posing as Farrell she then kills the crew of the Tiger, a state-of-the-art stealth helicopter which is NATO's latest deterrent, and pilots the aircraft out from under the noses of the French Navy.

The helicopter lands outside the Severnaya Station, a secret underground installation in Siberia which houses the Soviet space weapons research centre. Inside the centre, Xenia massacres the staff with her machine gun. Only two escape. Computer whizz-kid Boris Grishenko had been smoking a cigarette outside; he disappears. Natalya Fyodorovna Simonova, a computer programmer, had been in the kitchen; at the sound of the gunfire she hides in a storage cabinet.

Ourumov unlocks the arming device of the GoldenEye rogue satellite, Petya, and programmes it to fire at the station in a matter of minutes. He and Xenia take off again in the helicopter. In space, the satellite sheds its camouflage, revealing at its core a nuclear bomb, which explodes. A huge magnetic pulse from the explosion destroys the satellite dish on the control centre and also three MIGs, scrambled to investigate the blast. Natalya escapes through the roof of the centre into the freezing Arctic weather.

Back in England, Bond is briefed by the new, female, M. She tells him that both British and American satellites were knocked out in the nuclear blast, and that the GoldenEye is an electro-magnetic-pulse strike satellite which creates a radiation surge that destroys anything with an electronic circuit within a fifty-mile radius. Moscow have explained away the incident as an accident during a routine training exercise. M believes the Janus Syndicate are involved, and the only traceable link to them is Xenia Onatopp, although Bond's old enemy Ourumov is believed to have been responsible for the breakdown in security at Severnaya. James Bond is briefed to penetrate the local arms mafia in Russia, seek out Janus, reassure the current Kremlin leadership and somehow bring Ourumov to justice. However, M warns Bond there must be no personal vendetta – avenging Alec Trevelyan will not bring him back.

After a visit to see Q for some new death-defying gadgets, 007 flies to St Petersburg. With the help of CIA contact Jack Wade, he searches out erstwhile KGB controller turned weapons mogul, Valentin Zukovsky, and introduces himself by pressing cold steel to Zukovsky's temple. 'Walther PPK 7.6mm. Lethal at 100 paces,' says Zukovsky. 'Only three men I know use that gun . . . and I believe I've killed two of them. Welcome back, Commander Bond.'

Meanwhile, Natalya has made it to St Petersburg and tracing Boris through his computer E-Mail, manages to arrange an assignation with her erstwhile colleague. Before she can question him about his escape from Severnaya she is seized from behind by Xenia.

At the Grand St Petersburg Hotel, Bond senses the presence of an intruder in the steam room – Xenia. Following a brief but passionate struggle, he escapes her deathly grip and, holding a gun to her head, he demands to be taken to Janus.

Xenia drives Bond to an industrial park full of statues of former Soviet leaders, where a figure walks out from behind one of the massive bronze tributes which are stored there. One side of the man's face is scarred. He greets Bond with a sneer, calling him 'Her Majesty's loyal terrier'. It is Alec Trevelyan. Stunned, Bond begins to understand that Trevelyan is Janus, a descendant of the Lienz Cossacks, a group which had fought for the Nazis against Russia in the Second World War. At the end of the war they surrendered to the British, expecting to join their war against communism. Instead they were sent back to Stalin who executed them. Trevelyan explains that his parents had escaped the execution squads but committed suicide in

Opposite: **Hell's Angels watch out – the beautiful, and very dangerous, Xenia Onatopp (Famke Janssen).** Left above: **Xenia faces off against James Bond over the baccarat table.** Left below: **Natalya (Izabella Scorupco)** and computer whizz-kid **Boris Grishenko (Alan Cumming)** are startled by a discovery on their computer consoles. Below: **Samantha Bond becomes the third actress to portray Miss Moneypenny in the James Bond film series.**

shame. The British government had made the mistake of thinking Trevelyan must have been too young to remember. In Trevelyan's twisted imagination, Bond's failure to save him on their mission parallels the British government's treachery to his parents.

Suddenly a dart is fired into Bond's neck and he falls to the ground, unconscious. He comes round to find himself tied into a seat inside the Tiger helicopter, with Natalya shouting at him from the seat behind. Realising they are in the line of an incoming missile attack he head butts the control console and they are ejected to safety. They are picked up by Russian troops and questioned by Mishkin, the Russian Defence Minister. Natalya tells him that Ourumov was the traitor at Severnaya and that the explosion was set off by him – at which point Ourumov bursts in, grabs Bond's gun from the table and shoots Mishkin and his bodyguard dead.

Bond grabs the dead guard's Kalashnikov and blasts his way out of the building. Natalya is recaptured and bundled into a car driven by Ourumov. 007 commandeers a 36-ton Russian T55 tank and pursues them around St Petersburg, demolishing cars, statues and buildings in the chase. Ourumov manages to drag Natalya aboard Janus's mobile headquarters in a hyper-sophisticated armoured train, where they join Xenia and Trevelyan.

As the train moves off, Bond manoeuvres the tank into a railway tunnel, emerging to fire point blank at the oncoming engine; and as the train crashes into the tank, Bond enters the rear carriage and holds up Xenia and Trevelyan, who have been temporarily stunned by the impact of the crash. Ourumov enters with Natalya, holding a gun to her head. Bond shoots Ourumov dead but Xenia and Trevelyan escape. Armoured sheathing slams down over the windows. Bond has just three minutes to find a way out before the whole communication car detonates. Bond uses the laser beam in his watch to cut a hole in the armour-plated floor. Natalya manages to track the Janus command centre on its own computer network, just before she and Bond drop to freedom.

Acting on information from Trevelyan's computer, Bond and Natalya head for Cuba. On reconnaissance above the jungle, their light aircraft is disabled by a ground to air missile. 007 comes to a clearing at the edge of a lake, face to face with Xenia, who is harnessed and suspended from an attack helicopter. Bond opens fire, panicking the pilot who swerves away, thereby slamming Xenia into the fork of a tree where she is crushed to death.

Suddenly, a huge latticed structure rises from the centre of the lake, and the water recedes as a parabolic dish, one thousand feet in diameter, emerges from the lake bed. Bond and Natalya vault on to the dish and find themselves sliding helter-skelter towards the centre, dodging bullets shot by the guards who surround them. They hurtle out of control into the sump hole at the centre of the dish, which has easy access to the control centre itself. There they discover the true mission of Janus: to break into world banks by computer and transfer money electronically seconds before the one remaining GoldenEye satellite, Mischa, is set off to erase any record of the transactions. All the computer systems of the world's financial centres will go down, reducing global financial markets to nothing but blank screens.

In the ensuing battle, Boris discovers the Caribbean can be as cold as hell, and 007 finds he needs a head for heights for his final confrontation with Alec Trevelyan – a challenge which for 007 has become not only a matter of 'for Queen and Country' but also a very personal affair.

Natalya Simonova in GoldenEye is Izabella Scorupco's first English-speaking role. Born in 1970 in the Polish village of Byalystock, close to the Russian border, she lived there with her mother, a doctor. In 1978, they moved to a suburb outside Stockholm. Aged 17, Izabella became a teenage idol after appearing in a movie called *No One Can Love Like Us*. She developed her singing talent and her 1989 single, *Substitute*, and subsequent album, *Iza*, both reached gold in Sweden. In 1994, Izabella resumed acting and won the lead role in *Petri Tears* (1995).

Famke Janssen, who plays the deadly Xenia Onatopp, was born in Holland, began her professional career as a model, working at one time for Yves Saint Laurent. She now lives in the United States. After attending Columbia University and studying

Overleaf left: **Dressed to kill: Famke Janssen at Xenia Onatopp.** Overleaf right: **The casino gaming tables of the James Bond films have always been draped with a bevy of beauties, and *GoldenEye* is no exception to the rule.**

stagecraft with Harold Guskin, she moved to Los Angeles and appeared in television series such as *Melrose Place*. Her first starring role in a major motion picture was in *Lords of Illusion* (1995).

Actress Samantha Bond follows in the footsteps of Lois Maxwell and Caroline Bliss as the new Miss Moneypenny. Samantha is a member of the Royal Shakespeare Company and also played at the National Theatre in *The Cid*. She has also made many television appearances. *GoldenEye* follows her first feature film, *Erik the Viking*.

Serena Gordon – who plays Caroline, sent to Monte Carlo by M to evaluate Bond – trained at the Royal Academy of Dramatic Art in London, after which she joined the Regents Park Open Air Theatre Company, with whom she toured the Middle East. Her first film role was in the Merchant Ivory picture, *Maurice*, and she has appeared regularly on stage and on British television.

Minnie Driver, appearing as Irina the nightclub 'singer', attended the Webber Douglas Theatre School in London. She has made frequent appearances on British television, while her feature film appearances include *Circle of Friends, Sleepers, Big Night*, and *Grosse Point Blank* (1997).

Opposite: **Natalya Simonova (Izabella Scorupco) amid deadly nerve gas canisters. Below left: 007 meets weapons mogul Valentin Zukovsky in a nightclub, where the erstwhile KGB controller's girlfriend is the featured singer. Below: Irina (Minnie Driver), nightclub chanteuse.**

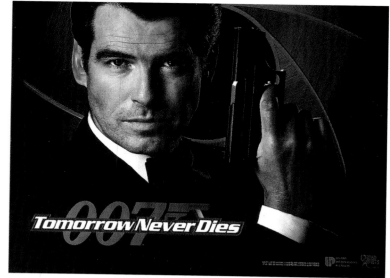

James Bond battles media mogul Elliot Carver in his apparent bid to start World War III.

After the British naval vessel *HMS Devonshire* has apparently been sunk by Chinese planes, M sends for agent 007. Studying a new language at Oxford University with linguist Professor Inga Bergstrom, 007 is telephoned by Miss Moneypenny. He is needed at the headquarters of the Ministry of Defence immediately. Agent 007's mission is to discover if a signal sent from one of Carver's communication satellites is involved with the sinking of the ship. Much to his displeasure, 007 is ordered to use his past relationship with Carver's wife, Paris, if it will aid the investigation. M tells 007 he has only forty-eight hours in which to prove the connection before Britain will take decisive action against the Chinese.

Arriving at Hamburg airport, Bond collects his hire car, a BMW 750i, from Q. He briefs Bond on its many gadgets, including a new cell phone which can operate the car by remote control, among other things. At Carver's party in his media headquarters, during which he will broadcast a declaration of his humanitarian principles, Bond, posing as a banker, meets the media mogul. The two men take an instant dislike to each other. Bond also meets an attractive oriental woman, Wai Lin, who says she's a reporter. During the party Bond manages to meet Paris in a quiet corner, where it is apparent to both of them that the embers of their relationship have far from cooled. As they return to the party they are greeted by Carver, who has noticed their discreet rendezvous. Bond realises that Paris is both frightened of, and desperate to please Carver. While Carver starts his TV broadcast Bond is given a tour of the building and is escorted into a recording studio where Carver's security guards attack him. 007 deals with the guards and pulls the circuit breakers on the CMGN newsroom, where the media mogul is cut off in mid-sentence as the newsroom is plunged into darkness.

Back in his hotel bedroom, Bond, gun in hand, waits apprehensively for the assailant that Carver will inevitably send. Bond is pleasantly surprised when Paris appears in the doorway. She has come to warn him that her husband is on to him. Their eyes lock and a passionate embrace follows. Later, Bond and Paris dress as she tells him about a secret laboratory on the top floor of the CMGN complex. Unknown to Bond and Paris, Carver's techno-terrorist associate, Henry Gupta, has played back their conversation from the security video to Carver. Checking Bond's employment record, Gupta believes it to be *too* perfect, pointing to him being a government agent.

James Bond	Pierce Brosnan
Elliot Carver	Jonathan Pryce
Wai Lin	Michelle Yeoh
Paris Carver	Teri Hatcher
Gupta	Ricky Jay
Stamper	Gotz Otto
Q	Desmond Llewelyn
Miss Moneypenny	Samantha Bond
Robinson	Colin Salmon
Admiral Roebuck	Geoffrey Palmer
General Bukharin	Terence Rigby
Minister of Defence	Julian Fellowes
Tamara Kelly	Nina Young
Professor Bergstrom	Cecilie Thomsen
Dr Kaufman	Vincent Schiavelli
Admiral Kelly	Michael Byrne
Avis Agent	Anjte Schmidt
and	
M	Judi Dench

Below left: **Carver's PR Officer (Daphne Deckers) introduces the media mogul on his world TV broadcast.** Below: **James Bond (Pierce Brosnan) and Paris Carver (Teri Hatcher), the ill-fated wife of media mogul Elliot Carver.** Opposite: **Wai Lin (Michelle Yeoh), a good ally when the going gets tough.**

Producers	Michael G. Wilson
	Barbara Broccoli
Director	Roger Spottiswoode
Story	Bruce Feirstein
Screenplay	Bruce Feirstein
Production Designer	Allan Cameron
Director of Photography	Robert Elswit
Line Producer	Anthony Waye

While investigating the secret laboratory Bond is unaware that Carver and Stamper, the vicious head of CMGN security, have ordered the murder of Paris. Bond escapes from the laboratory after finding Wai Lin also breaking into the complex. She leaves in spectacular style as 007 takes on a number of Stamper's security guards. Bond has taken a GPS encoder from the lab safe, equipment which could have been involved in sending a misleading signal to *HMS Devonshire*. Returning to his hotel room, he is overwhelmed with grief and anger at finding Paris strangled in his bed. A soft voice from the bathroom snaps 007 out of his immediate grief. It is Dr Kaufman, a hired killer who specialises in making murder look like suicide. Carver has planned to make Bond the suicide victim in his murder/suicide plot to shift blame for his wife's murder. When Stamper phones Kaufman to get Bond to open his heavily protected BMW in the hotel car park, 007 tricks the murderous doctor into using Q's ingenious cell phone so that the stun gun inside goes off in his hands. Giving Bond the edge he needed, he shoots Kaufman dead with his own gun. Bond escapes after an amazing car chase in the hotel multi-storey car park involving 007's BMW.

Landing at a US air force base in Okinawa, Commander James Bond RN has brought the GPS encoder with him to seek advice from the air force's expert, Dr Greenwalt. The scientist explains to Bond that, in theory, if someone altered the timing chip in the decoder it could slowly send a ship off course – similar to putting a magnet next to a compass. Checking on the *Devonshire's* last position, they calculate exactly where she sank. 007 parachutes into the sea in search of the sunken Royal Naval vessel.

Bond discovers *HMS Devonshire* 200 feet below on the ocean floor, with a large hole literally drilled in her hull, and Wai Lin investigating the wreck. They barely escape with their lives as the ship slides into a deep sea trench. Returning to the surface they are captured by Stamper and his men. Handcuffed together, Bond and Wai Lin are flown to Carver's Saigon headquarters. Outside Carver's office they are passed in the corridor by Chinese soldiers in civilian clothes, and a Chinese man with an air of military command. Wai Lin registers great alarm. She covers it – but not before Bond has seen her reaction. They are brought before Carver, who is sitting at a computer screen writing their obituaries: 'British Secret Service Agent James Bond and his collaborator Wai Lin of the Chinese People's External Security Force were found dead today in Vietnam.' Bond realises Carver is quite insane. The media mogul hopes to achieve global domination by influencing the minds of people over the entire world through his media empire which, after the final part of his plan is put into effect, will have more people under his influence than anyone else has achieved in the history of the planet. Carver leaves Bond and Wai Lin in the sadistic hands of Stamper, who prepares to torture them to death. Before

Stamper can use a selection of grotesque surgical instruments on the couple, they shatter a window and leap for their lives. Landing on a deck one storey below, Bond and Wai Lin, holding the ropes from a banner, take an unbelievable leap over the edge of the building, ripping the banner, which slows their descent as they fall. Still handcuffed together, Bond and Wai Lin elude Stamper's security men on a motorcycle, while they are strafed by a helicopter, in a wild chase from boat to boat, through streets, houses, open-air markets, and over rooftops. Discovering that an innocent-looking bicycle repair shop is in fact a communications and supply depot for renegade Chinese soldiers, 007 and Wai Lin deduce the location of the craft which Carver has used to sink *HMS Devonshire*. It is a 'stealth' boat, completely invisible to radar and built with the help of General Chang, who had, as Wai Lin discovered a year earlier, stolen material essential for its construction. Before they leave, 007 and Wai Lin send a warning message to Beijing via computer, and leave for Ha Long Bay.

In their Zodiac dinghy, Bond and Wai Lin cruise into the cove where they discover the state-of-the-art 'stealth' boat with its smooth planed surfaces and an utterly black

Opposite: **Paris Carver (Teri Hatcher)** is classy, sophisticated, and sexy: three attributes that no one would argue with concerning this lady. Left above: **Language Professor, Bergstrom (Cecilia Thomsen)** enlarges 007's vocabulary. Left below: **Paris Carver** causes the displeasure of her husband Elliot **(Jonathan Pryce)**, and doesn't live to tell the tale. Below: **Cecilia Thomsen** brings a different meaning to the word 'Professor'.

finish. On board, Carver and Gupta prepare to instigate an unprovoked attack. 007 and Wai Lin board the craft and begin planting limpet mines, when Carver picks her up on the security video monitors. Stamper grabs Wai Lin and Bond goes after her. The 'stealth' boat moves into position between the British and Chinese fleets and fires a small missile at the flagship of each fleet. The ships zigzag at high speed to avoid the missiles, which explode in the water just beyond. In response, the Chinese scramble a squadron of MIGs, while on board the British flagship *HMS Bedford*, Admiral Kelly orders the launch of a harpoon missile as a warning shot. Carver orders Stamper to bring Wai Lin to him on the bridge. While removing the limpet mines hidden by the two secret agents, Stamper shoots a guard dressed by 007 in his own clothes. Believing he has killed Bond, Stamper returns to the bridge. Carver explains to Wai Lin that there are only nine short minutes before the Chinese MIGs will attack the British fleet, and then he will fire the cruise missile he has stolen from the wreck of the *Devonshire*. 007 makes a bomb from a flare and two oxygen canisters, and primes it with a detonator from his watch, and then wedges the device between two heat exchangers. With 'Air Threat Warning Red' on board *HMS Bedford*, Bond has little time to put his back-up plan into effect. 007 makes his way into Gupta's control room. Holding the man at gunpoint, he overhears Carver lecturing Wai Lin over the intercom.

Meanwhile back in England, M, without ceremony, bursts into the MOD Situation Room to inform the Minister of Defence that she's just confirmed a message from 007 via her opposite number in Beijing. Their ships should look for a boat invisible to radar. The Chinese are not the enemy: Carver has been playing both sides for fools.

Carver's intention has been that the Chinese leaders will be killed and General Chang will take over the government, negotiate a truce, and give him exclusive broadcasting rights in China for the next fifty years. Believing that Carver needs Gupta to launch the cruise missile, 007 attempts to exchange him for Wai Lin. When Gupta tells Carver the missile is ready for launch, he seals his own fate. Gesturing to Stamper for a weapon, Carver shoots Gupta dead. Simultaneously Bond activates his back-up plan: he presses the sweep button on his watch and the upper stern platform wall of the launch bay explodes with shattering force. 007 grabs Wai Lin as Carver is blown backwards by the blast, which has breached the hull enabling the fleets to see the 'stealth' boat on radar.

Bond and Wai Lin take on the media mogul and his crew in a battle to the death – in which 007 teaches Carver and Stamper a new definition of 'dead in the water'.

In keeping with the independent, self-assured, sexually confident woman of today, the main heroine of *Tomorrow Never Dies*, Colonel Wai Lin, as portrayed by Michelle Yeoh, is a perfect reflection of the modern woman, and is a formidable ally for secret agent 007, certainly matching him talent for talent.

Michelle was born Yeoh Choo Kheng in Ipoh, Malaysia. While in high school she was active in sports, and represented Malaysia in squash, diving and swimming competitions. Her passion for ballet led her to enrol in the Royal Academy of Dance in London, where she attained an Advanced Level degree. Eventually she received a Bachelor of Arts degree in Creative Arts in England. But her ballet career was cut short by an injury. In 1983 she returned to Malaysia and entered a beauty pageant. She was crowned Miss Malaysia, as well as 'Miss Mooba' in Melbourne the same year.

In 1984 she was invited to Hong Kong to make a commercial with Jackie Chan. Instantly, she became the most sought-after new talent in the movie industry. She signed with D&B Films and made her debute in 1985 in a non-action role in the action comedy *Owls Vs. Dumbo*. It was her second film, *Yes Madam*, which established her as the premiere female action star in Asia. Her next two pictures, *Royal Warriors* (also known as *In The Line of Duty*) and *Magnificent Warriors*, further fortified her position. Her training in dance contributed to one of the unique characteristics of her acting talent – she performed her own stunts! In 1988, after only one more picture, *Easy Money*, she married and retired from the screen.

Her marriage lasted four years. Then she made an astonishing comeback. *Police Story III: Supercop*, co-starring Jackie Chan, was the top-grossing film in Asia in 1992 and Michelle became the most popular and the highest-paid actress in Asia. Typical of her stunt work is a high speed motorcycle jump onto the roof of a fast-moving train in

Supercop. In the next two years she made a total of eight pictures, including cult classics *The Heroic Trio* and *Tai-chi Master*.

In 1995 she decided to expand her acting scope and starred in two dramatic films in a row: the period epic *The Soong Sisters* and *The Story of Ah Gum*.

In addition to her film activities, Michelle is also a committee member of the Hong Kong Cancer Fund and Honorary Patron of KELY Support Group.

Every James Bond movie has its 'sacrificial lamb', and *Tomorrow Never Dies* is no exception. Played with style and aplomb by American actress Teri Hatcher, Paris Carver is an ex-lover of James Bond, who falls foul of her mad media mogul husband, Elliot Carver, whose penalty for betrayal is death.

Teri has emerged as one of the most sought-after talents on both the large and small screens. Towards the end of 1996 she earned widespread praise as part of the ensemble cast of the critically acclaimed MGM release *2 Days In The Valley*. Her other film credits include a provocative role in the erotic thriller *Heaven's Prisoners*, with Alec Baldwin and Eric Roberts. She also appeared opposite David Schwimmer in his directorial debut film *Since You've Been Gone*. She made her feature film debut in the Hollywood satire *The Big Picture*, starring Kevin Bacon, and her earlier work also includes a memorable part in the comedy *Soapdish*, starring Sally Field and Kevin Kline.

She is probably most well known for her role as the savvy and sophisticated Lois Lane in the ABC TV series *Lois & Clark: The New Adventures of Superman*, an international hit shown in more than 35 countries. She has a huge following in the United States, and her fan sites on the Internet number over 7,000.

Opposite: **Asia's top action star Michelle Yeoh brings femininity as well as toughness to her role as Wai Lin.** Below left: **Agent 007 (Pierce Brosnan) catches Wai Lin breaking into Gupta's secret laboratory.** Below: **Moneypenny (Samantha Bond) telephones 007 and tells him M requires his presence immediately.** Following pages: **James Bond is pleased to be working with such a tactile partner as Wai Lin. Paris Carver (Teri Hatcher) visits Bond in his hotel room. Handcuffed together, Bond and Wai Lin escape from Carver's thugs on a motorcycle.**